W9-CCR-661

WORD
BIBLICAL
THEMES

WORD BIBLICAL THEMES

1 Peter

J. RAMSEY MICHAELS

WORD PUBLISHING
Dallas · London · Sydney · Singapore

1 Peter

Word Biblical Themes

Quotations from the Scriptures in this volume are the author's own translation unless otherwise indicated.

Library of Congress Cataloging-in-Publication Data

Michaels, J. Ramsey
   1 Peter / J. Ramsey Michaels.
      p.   cm. — (Word Biblical themes)
   Includes bibliographical references.
    1. Bible. N.T. Peter, 1st—Criticism, interpretation, etc.
  I. Title. II. Title: First Peter. III. Series.
BS2795.2.M53 1989
227'.9206—dc20   89-37586
                                               CIP

Printed in the United States of America
9 8 0 1 2 3 9 RRD 9 8 7 6 5 4 3 2 1

To my colleagues in Religious Studies at
Southwest Missouri State University,
with gratitude, affection, and respect.

CONTENTS

FOREWORD

Finding the great themes of the books of the Bible is essential to the study of God's Word and to the preaching and teaching of its truths. These themes and ideas are often like precious gems: they lie beneath the surface and can only be discovered with some difficulty. Commentaries are most useful to this discovery process, but they are not usually designed to help the reader to trace important subjects systematically within a given book of Scripture.

This series, Word Biblical Themes, addresses this need by bringing together, within a few pages, all of what is contained in a biblical book on the subjects that are thought to be most significant to that book. A companion series to the Word Biblical Commentary, this series distills the theological essence of a book of Scripture as interpreted in the more technical series and serves it up in ways that will enrich the preaching, teaching, worship, and discipleship of God's people.

The New Testament document known as 1 Peter claims a distinctive place in the library of the church's canon. It represents an attractive and insightful bid to describe what the Christian life is meant to be in times of stress. Its theology is practical and down-to-earth; its tone and temper is that of applied Christianity.

For this reason, above all, it makes a special appeal to the preacher and Bible class teacher. Many congregations and study groups will respond positively to the exposition of this letter, with contemporary relevance not far to seek.

Professor J. Ramsey Michaels has already put the scholarly world in his debt by his thorough and suggestive commentary in the Word Biblical Commentary series. Now he offers a fresh range of insights and suggestions designed to stimulate further reflection and to assist pastors and teachers along with their groups in the understanding of this short, fascinating epistle.

This book is brimful of ideas and hints, based on a careful study of the setting of 1 Peter, intended to make the letter meaningful in today's church and world.

Ralph P. Martin
Department of Biblical Studies
The University of Sheffield

PREFACE

Many years ago one of my students remarked enthusiastically that he considered the first epistle of Peter a real "potboiler." I did not have the heart to correct him. In fact, since he was British, I assumed he must have known of some obscure secondary meaning of the term "potboiler" that was unfamiliar to me. Because he is now a distinguished colleague teaching in an overseas seminary, he shall remain nameless.

As I reflected on my friend's misuse of words, I realized that the term "potboiler" actually does evoke some of the true characteristics of 1 Peter. I presume my friend was trying to tell me that he found 1 Peter "packed" or "loaded" with meaning and rich, powerful insights into the work of Christ and the responsibilities of Christian believers—like a "pot boiling over." If that is what he meant, he was not far off the mark. The imagery was there even though the word was not quite right.

My own study of 1 Peter over the years, both devotional and scholarly, has only deepened my sense of wonder at the richness of this brief letter attributed to the prince of

Apostles. It was a rare privilege for me, therefore, to contribute a volume on 1 Peter to the Word Biblical Commentary series (1988). The completion of the project has not diminished my fascination with this letter, nor has familiarity dampened my appreciation of its unique testimony to Christ and Christian living. On the contrary, it has increased them immeasurably. Now I am grateful to Ralph Martin and Word Publishing for the opportunity to highlight some major themes of 1 Peter for a somewhat wider audience in the present volume.

1 Peter is seldom listed among the major witnesses of the New Testament. It has not received the scholarly attention given to Paul—what is one short letter weighed against a dozen?—nor the attention given to any of the Gospels, or the Book of Acts, or even the Book of Revelation. It has never challenged the great preachers of the church in quite the same way that the letter to the Romans or the Gospel of John challenged them. This is surprising in view of the fact that its author is supposed to have been the one to whom Jesus gave "the keys of the kingdom of heaven" and the promise that "whatever you bind on earth shall be bound in heaven, and whatever you loose on earth shall be loosed in heaven" (Matt 16:19).

One reason for the comparative neglect of 1 Peter in the church and in the academy is its brevity, and another is its association with 2 Peter, which is almost certainly not the work of the Apostle Peter but the product of the next generation in the development of the ancient church. Doubtless some of the uncertainty about the authorship of 2 Peter has rubbed off on 1 Peter in the eyes of scholars. And as long as the need exists to interpret 1 and 2 Peter under a common rubric, the distinctiveness of each is to some degree going to be lost. Once 1 Peter is separated from 2 Peter and Jude, and from the broad miscellaneous category of "Catholic Epistles" or "General Epistles," so as to be appreciated in its own right as a unique witness to Jesus Christ, its stock rises.

This is precisely what has happened, by editorial decision, in the Word Biblical Commentary and Word Biblical Themes series. For example, 1 and 2 Corinthians were put together in a single volume in the themes series (though not of course in the commentary) because their themes and the situations they presupposed were intertwined. This is not the case with 1 and 2 Peter, and the editors wisely decided (despite their brevity) to keep them separate in both series. For this, readers have every reason to be grateful.

There is no one correct way to bring out the major themes of even a short letter such as 1 Peter. From a purely theological standpoint, it can be done in relation to the Trinity—God, Christ, and the Spirit—as I attempted to do in the last few pages of the introduction to the commentary (pp. lxvii-lxxv). In the present volume I have chosen instead to set forth the perspective of 1 Peter on the past, the present, and the future of the people of God, with special attention to the transition from present to future. For this idea (though not for its application to 1 Peter) I am indebted to Bruce J. Malina, whose thought-provoking article, "Christ and Time: Swiss or Mediterranean?" appeared in the *Catholic Biblical Quarterly* in January 1989.

I have also made generous use, where appropriate, of the thoughts and language of Christian poets and literary figures, among them Gerard Manley Hopkins, Gilbert K. Chesterton, Flannery O'Connor, C. S. Lewis, and Amos Wilder, and of the language of certain familiar hymns and gospel songs. I have learned through the years that the books of the New Testament are not only full of words but of music as well. The tools of biblical exegesis help us to get the words right, but if we want to hear the Word of God in all its power and fullness we must listen to the music. Few New Testament books are richer in their music than 1 Peter, and sometimes the writers and poets can help us hear notes we might otherwise miss.

If the wording of my quotations from 1 Peter seems unfamiliar, it is because I am using my own translation from the commentary. The reader will not go far wrong, however, with the RSV or the NIV. Comparison with the translation used in this volume may even be illuminating. At 1 Pet 4:14, however, the longer text followed by the King James Version is to be preferred over all the rest. Those who are looking for bibliography, or for discussions of alternative views on various questions of interpretation in 1 Peter will not find such information here. For this, they are referred to the commentary. The information explosion in biblical studies is such that even there only a sampling is possible.

It is my hope that this modest volume might contribute in its way to the renewal of the Christian church in our time. Whether it does or not depends on whether it falls into the hands of someone who will catch the spirit—not of this book, to be sure, but of 1 Peter itself—and help bring to realization Peter's vision of what it means to be the people of God in a world and a culture still far from God, the Father of Jesus Christ our Lord.

1 THE AUTHOR AND READERS OF 1 PETER

The apostle and his letter

A quick survey of all the letters contained in the New Testament gives the impression that Paul had something close to a copyright on the title, "apostle of Jesus Christ [or Christ Jesus]." No less than five of his letters begin with this self-designation, while in four others he begins by referring to his apostleship in some way. The only other New Testament figure to call himself an apostle is Peter in the two letters attributed to him: "Peter, apostle of Jesus Christ" (1 Pet 1:1); "Symeon Peter, servant and apostle of Jesus Christ" (2 Pet 1:1). Other writings *may* of course have been written by apostles—the gospels of Matthew and John, the three letters of John, Hebrews, and Revelation—but none of these make an *explicit* claim to that effect (at most there is an implicit, though anonymous, apostolic claim at the beginning of 1 John). With respect to *literary self-consciousness*, there seem to have been only two apostles, Peter and Paul.

If the apostolic claims of 1–2 Peter are accepted, then

these two letters are a precious legacy from one very close to Jesus who was given the "keys of the kingdom of heaven," judicial authority to "bind and loose" in the church (Matt 16:19), and the responsibility to "feed" or "shepherd" Jesus' followers (John 21:15-17). Many of the ancient church fathers had serious doubts as to whether 2 Peter came directly from Peter's hand—or even from Peter's lifetime—and most modern scholars share those doubts, but the claims of 1 Peter are taken far more seriously. Though it is widely acknowledged that Peter the Galilean fisherman whose first language was Aramaic may have had some secretarial help in composing this elegant epistle in Greek, there is little reason to doubt that the ideas are Peter's own and that the life situation addressed is one that Peter himself could have faced. Unlike 2 Peter, 1 Peter was generally known and accepted in the church from the early second century on. Its claim to authenticity is strong.

In view of all this it is surprising that 1 Peter has occupied such a modest place in the New Testament in comparison with the letters of Paul. This can be attributed in part to its brevity, in part to its association with the less widely accepted 2 Peter, and in part to its superficial resemblance to the letters of Paul. If a person's expectation of what a New Testament letter should be is shaped entirely by Paul's letters, the tendency is to regard 1 Peter as if the author were trying to be like Paul but not quite succeeding! Where, some have asked, is justification by faith? Where are the great debates over the law? Where are the memorable Pauline themes of the body of Christ and life in the Spirit? When Paul's letters are allowed to set the agenda, 1 Peter is not properly appreciated. On the other hand, when 1 Peter is read for itself, its own rich contribution to Christian life and thought becomes readily apparent. No one will argue that the significance of 1 Peter outweighs that of the thirteen letters attributed to Paul. Yet significance is not measured by length. The value of 1 Peter lies in the fact that it represents "another voice" besides Paul's, a voice of one speaking, no less than Paul, as an "apostle of Jesus Christ."

The opening of 1 Peter establishes once and for all Peter's apostolic authority over his readers, and he has no need to invoke that authority again. Instead, he builds common ground with his readers as "fellow elder" to those who give leadership to their congregations (5:1). With the elders he testifies to the sufferings of Jesus Christ on the cross, and he shares with elders and all believers in the coming glory of Christ's return. Peter does not command his readers to do what *he* wants, but rather "appeals" to them to fulfill their own calling as the people of God (cf. 2:11). His letter is neither a manifesto nor a book of rules, but a gift—nothing less than "true grace from God" (5:12). For the most part he allows his words to stand on their own merit, without constantly reminding the congregations of who he is or of the authority with which he writes.

Peter, "rock" and shepherd

Who then was "Peter"? The answer seems simple enough. In the gospels, he is "Simon, son of John," a Galilean fisherman who answered the call of Jesus, and at some point—either at his call (John 1:42) or later, when he recognized Jesus as Messiah (Matt 16:18)—acquired the nickname "Cephas" (Aramaic) or "Peter" (Greek), meaning "Rock." Jesus tells him, "You are Peter, and on this rock [*petra*] I will build my congregation" (Matt 16:18). In view of Jesus' parable about the wisdom of "building on the rock" (Matt 7:24-25), it appears that Jesus is conferring on "Peter" a great honor. Yet there is irony in the pronouncement too because in a few short verses Peter will be unable to accept the prospect of Jesus' suffering and death, and Jesus will say to him, "Get back in line, Satan! You are a scandal to me, for your concern is not with the things of God, but with human things" (Matt 16:23). Six days later, at the Transfiguration, "Peter the Rock" will say, without thinking, "Rabbi, it is good for us to be here; let us make three tabernacles, one for you and one for Moses and one for Elijah" (Matt 17:4 // Mark 9:5-6). When Jesus is arrested, Peter, despite all his claims to the contrary (Matt 26:33 // Mark 14:29), will desert Jesus with the rest of the disciples. When asked about his relationship to Jesus, he will deny three times that any such relationship exists. In light of these subsequent events, there is indeed irony in Jesus' designation of Simon as "Peter," the Rock. Some "rock" this fearful disciple turned out to be! All talk, and no action! Peter is not heard from again in Matthew and is mentioned in Mark only when the angel commands the women at the tomb to tell his disciples "and Peter" that Jesus will regather the scattered disciples and lead them back to Galilee (Mark 16:7; cf. 14:27).

In John's Gospel there is a reunion in Galilee, and Peter does play a conspicuous part in that reunion. In some respects he is rehabilitated. His three affirmations of love for Jesus (John 21:15-17) can be read as the undoing of his threefold denial—both taking place in the light and warmth of a "charcoal fire" (21:9; cf. 18:18). He is given a new role as shepherd of Jesus' flock with the repeated command, "Feed my lambs. . . . Tend my sheep. . . . Feed my sheep." Yet there is irony even in Peter's rehabilitation. He fails to recognize the risen Jesus by the lake in Galilee until the anonymous "disciple whom Jesus loved" tells him, "It is the Lord" (21:7). He is later rebuked for being too curious about the subsequent fate of the beloved disciple (21:20-22). The setting is Jesus' solemn prediction of Peter's death (introduced by "Truly, truly, I say to you," 21:18), but even this pronouncement is not without irony. It is a prophecy, to be sure, but a prophecy couched in the form of a riddle:

"When you were young, you girded yourself and walked wherever you wanted, but when you are old, you will stretch out your hands and another will gird you and take you where you do not want to go."

If this is said "to show by what death Peter was to glorify God" (John 21:19), what kind of death was it, the heroic death of a martyr or the natural death of a feeble old man unable to dress himself? Later Christian tradition decided for the former, but the saying itself leaves the issue unresolved. The death of any true believer "glorifies God," but the prophecy does little to illumine the exact circumstances of Peter's death. If he was a martyr, he was an unwilling one, taken "where you do not want to go," and not the kind who follows the precedent of Jesus in "laying down his life" freely (John 10:17-18). The latter was what he had claimed when he said to Jesus earlier, "I will lay down my life for you" (13:37), but the fulfillment (if it is that) falls short of the aspiration. Tradition has made of Peter a heroic martyr in the time of the persecution of the church by Nero in A.D. 64, but there is no biblical evidence to support this. The alternatives often proposed, that 1 Peter is either written before 64 or else is written by someone other than Peter, should not be accepted as the only possible alternatives. A third possibility is that Peter lived into the seventies, perhaps even the eighties, and died an unremarkable death. If so, the letter we know as 1 Peter may well be the work of his later years.

The glimpses of Peter provided by Mark, Matthew, and John suggest that Peter was not consistently a noble or heroic figure in early Christianity. There was in his earnest and impetuous pronouncements something all too human, even at times faintly comic. He is taken more seriously, however, in Luke's Gospel (e.g., 22:31-33; 24:34) and in the Book of Acts, where his sermons, miracles, and visions mark decisive steps in the expansion of the early church (e.g., Acts 2:14-36; 3:1-10; 10:9-16, 34-43). He is also taken more seriously, as we

The Author and Readers of 1 Peter

would expect, in the two New Testament letters attributed to him. Here the irony of Matthew, Mark, and John is remembered but not perpetuated. In 2 Peter he is represented as being aware of his own impending death, but with no hint that it is to be a martyr's death or in any way particularly heroic (2 Pet 1:13–14). In 1 Peter he recalls the imagery of a "rock" or "stone" as the foundation of Christian faith and life (1 Pet 2:4–8), but without reference to himself. The "living Stone" on which the temple of God is built is unmistakably Christ himself. His reminder that Christ "the foundation of the corner" is for unbelievers "a stone for stumbling and a rock to trip over" (Greek: *petra skandalou*, lit., "rock of scandal," 2:8) may even contain a wry echo of Jesus' stinging rebuke to him years before, "You are a scandal to me" (Matt 16:23). The irony is there, and he lets it stand, but he calls no attention to it. In 5:1–4 Peter assigns to the elders of the congregations to which he writes the role of shepherd ("Shepherd the flock of God that is in your care," v 2). To the extent that he is their "fellow elder" (v 1), he too is a shepherd, but he assigns no uniqueness to his own role. He and they alike await the appearing of Christ, the "chief shepherd" (v 4), to whom all shepherds and sheep are finally accountable (cf. 2:25). In short, Peter makes nothing of the prerogatives assigned to him, whether ironically or in all seriousness, in the gospels. Though he bears the authority of an "apostle of Jesus Christ" in 1 Peter, he writes this letter as one of us, a man who lives in the same world we do, subject to the same aggravations and prone to the same kinds of mistakes. Because of this, and not in spite of it, we do well to ponder his words carefully, even across the span of nineteen centuries.

The original readers of the letter

To whom was 1 Peter written? Obviously to Christians who recognized and valued Peter's authority. According to indictment makes it unmistakably clear that Peter has in mind Gentile Christians who turned from idolatry to the worship of one God and to faith in Jesus Christ (cf. Paul in 1 Thess 1:9–10). 1 Peter is best understood, therefore, as a circular or "diaspora" letter addressed to an undetermined number of gentile Christian congregations in five Roman provinces of Asia Minor: "Pontus, Cappadocia, Galatia, Asia, and Bithynia" (1:1). The list begins and ends with provinces bordering the Black Sea, and it appears that the order in which the provinces are listed roughly describes the itinerary or "postal route" to be followed by the person delivering the letter (probably Silvanus, 5:12).

Why would Peter address communities of Gentile Christians as if they were Jews? He does so for two reasons, one related to the past, the other to the present. The first is that he wants to give them a new heritage—a whole new past— to replace the "empty way of life that was your heritage" (1:18), and the only heritage he can give them is his own, the heritage of the Jews and Judaism. The second is that he wants to underscore certain real parallels between their experience and the experience of the Jews, above all the experience of being "aliens and strangers" in the cities and provinces where they live (2:11). These two purposes will be the subject matter of the next two chapters. Only by reading 1 Peter through the eyes of those Gentile Christians to whom it was first directed can we understand its message to us, and to the different—yet not so different—situations we face today.

Paul's account in Galatians, it was agreed that Paul had been "entrusted with the task of preaching the gospel to the Gentiles just as Peter had been to the Jews" (Gal 2:7). This would suggest that the proper sphere of Peter's mission and pastoral concern was Jewish Christianity. Yet Peter in the Book of Acts is portrayed as the first to bring the Christian message to Gentiles (Acts 10:9-16, 44-48). At the council in Jerusalem he claims that "in the early days God determined that by my mouth the Gentiles should hear the word of the gospel and believe" (Acts 15:7).

Which group is the implied audience of 1 Peter? Here too the signals are mixed. Right at the outset the readers are addressed as "a chosen people, living as strangers in the diaspora of Pontus, Galatia, Cappadocia, Asia, and Bithynia" (1:1). Such terms as "chosen people" and "diaspora" suggest a Jewish (i.e., Jewish Christian) audience. The word "diaspora" is still used today for the Jewish community scattered throughout the whole world. The beginning of 1 Peter calls to mind the Jewish Christian letter of James, addressed to "the twelve tribes of the diaspora" (James 1:1). This impression is heightened later in the letter when Peter calls his readers "a chosen race, the King's priesthood, a holy nation" (2:9) and refers to those outside their number as "Gentiles" (2:12; 4:3).

Yet at the same time the readers are described in ways that would hardly have been appropriate if they were actually Jews. Peter refers to their life before they knew Christ as a life of "ignorance" (1:14). Whatever their failures, the Jews were hardly ignorant of God or of the laws of God. No first-century Christian, Jewish or gentile, would have described Judaism as "the empty way of life that was your heritage" (1:18). No group of Jews would ever have been depicted as having once done "what the Gentiles wanted, as you went along with them in acts of immorality and lust, drunken orgies, feasts, revelries, and lawless acts of idolatry" (4:3). Individuals might have done so, of course, but such a blanket

2   THE PAST: CLAIMING A HERITAGE

What exactly was the "Jewish heritage" Peter wanted his Gentile readers to claim for their own, and on what basis was it theirs? These questions can be answered with respect to three aspects of Jewish identity: *first*, the Scripture; *second*, Jewish stories, both oral and written, and the heroes and heroines of those stories; *third*, the Messiah. These are obviously not all there is to Judaism, either in Peter's day or our own. Peter says nothing of Jewish laws, whether about food, the Sabbath, the temple, circumcision, or ritual purity. Consciously or not, he avoids the thorny issues addressed at the Jerusalem Council in Acts 15, the issues that divided Paul from his opponents in Galatians. He has nothing to say to the question of whether Gentile converts to Christianity must be circumcised and eat kosher food. Either these debates had been settled in accordance with the decree sent to the gentile churches and recorded in Acts 15:23-29, or they simply held no interest for Peter at the time he wrote the letter. 1 Peter is more interested in Jewish identity and in the stake that even gentile Christians have in it rather than in the details of Jewish practice.

The book

Judaism is routinely called a religion of the book, though it is far more than that. When Gentiles in the first century began to "turn to God from idols, to serve the living and true God, and to wait for his Son from heaven" (1 Thess 1:9-10), it was by no means inevitable that they would embrace the Jewish Scriptures along with Jesus, the Jewish Messiah. These Scriptures, after all, were the work of a foreign people and had been translated into Greek from a strange barbarian tongue. They did not mention Jesus explicitly, and they went on and on about alien and primitive laws and customs. In the second century, some Gentile Christians would try to eliminate passages that seemed irrelevant or inappropriate, and some would dispense with the Jewish Scriptures altogether. The most extreme of these was Marcion, from Sinope in Pontus on the Black Sea, within the circle of churches to which 1 Peter had been written. Yet long before Marcion, several of the New Testament writers—among them Matthew, Paul, John, and Peter—quoted freely from the Jewish Scriptures, which they were coming to regard as the "Old Testament," in order to show that these ancient and foreign-sounding documents pointed unmistakably to Jesus as Messiah of the Jews and Lord and Savior of the Gentiles. Their intent in finding Jesus Christ in the Jewish Scriptures was not only to proclaim Jesus Christ but to commend these Scriptures to Gentile Christians as true revelation from God, "profitable for teaching, for reproof, for correction, and for training in righteousness" (2 Tim 3:16).

1 Peter is part of this early concern to promote respect for the Jewish Scriptures among Gentile Christians. Peter does this by explicit citations from the psalms and the prophets, often introduced by the formula, "It is written." These citations are not mere footnotes to his argument that readers

might take seriously or ignore as they choose. Rather, the citations come at crucial points in the letter and contribute significantly to Peter's argument. Without them, 1 Peter would not be the letter it is, and perhaps not even a coherent piece of correspondence. For example, in 1:13-21, the heart of Peter's positive commands to his readers is found in vv 15-16: "like the Holy One who called you, be holy in all your conduct, for *it is written*, 'Be holy because I am holy.'" First comes the application of the text and then the text itself, in this case Lev 19:2 (cf. also Lev 11:44; 20:7, 26). In 1:22-25 he makes the point that Christian love is unremitting and eternal because the Christian gospel is eternal. This time he introduces the citation abruptly, with "for" (literally, "be-cause") instead of "It is written": "For 'all humanity is like grass, and all its glory like the wild flower; the grass withers and the flower falls away, but *what the Lord has said* endures forever.' *What he has said* is the message of the gospel that has been proclaimed to you" (vv 24-25). Here Peter does not claim explicitly to be quoting from a written text (though he is in fact quoting Isa 40:6-8), nor does it matter to his argu-ment whether he is or not. The last sentence makes it clear in any case that the "word of the Lord," which created flowers and grass and mortal flesh and will endure long after they are gone, is the same as the "word of the gospel" preached some years before to these Christians in Asia Minor (cf. 1:12). Be-cause of this, the readers of this letter are children of the Creator and Sustainer of the universe. If we have accepted the Christian gospel, we have both a past and a future. Our lives are shaped neither by the changing cycles of nature nor by the whims of society and its rulers, but by the will of "the living and enduring God" (v 23).

In 2:6, Peter resumes the practice of quoting Scripture explicitly: "For it says in writing, 'Behold I am laying a choice and precious stone, a cornerstone in Zion, and the person who believes in him will never be put to shame'" (cf. Isa

28:16). The citation affords him the opportunity to draw into his argument in a more informal way two other texts, Ps 118:22 ("the stone which the builders rejected has become the foundation of the corner") and Isa 8:14 ("a stone for stumbling and a rock to trip over"). All three texts have in common the word "stone," and Peter's argument is that the "stone" to which they all refer is Jesus Christ. He interprets his texts already in 2:4-5, before citing even the first of them: "As you come to him, the living Stone, rejected by people generally but in God's sight choice and precious, you yourselves, like living stones, are being built into a spiritual house for holy priesthood, to offer up spiritual sacrifices acceptable to God through Jesus Christ."

Peter's procedure is the same as in 1:15-16: first the interpretation of the text, then the text itself. This order probably reflects the experience of the Gentile Christians to whom Peter was writing: first they met Jesus Christ in the proclaimed message; then they found him (with the help of Peter and other Jewish Christians) in the Jewish Scriptures. It also reflects the experience of many Christians today. Once we have come to know Jesus Christ as Lord and become part of a serious Christian community, we discover prophecies and promises of him in the Old Testament. Finding Christ in the Old Testament is a favorite pastime of Christian interpreters. For Peter, however, even the discovery of Jesus Christ in the Jewish Scriptures is not an end in itself or something he does in order to score points in debates with the Jews over the meaning of their Bible. Rather, his intent is to make a point about Christian identity. The real question he addresses is not "Who is Jesus Christ?" but "Who are we?" If Jesus is the "living Stone" mentioned in the two passages from Isaiah and the one from the Psalms, then we who belong to him are "living stones" (2:5).

Peter's metaphor of "living stones" is important not for itself (as, e.g., in John the Baptist's statement that "God is able from these stones to raise up children to Abraham" [Matt 3:9 // Luke 3:8]) but in relation to the metaphor of a temple. Like Paul (cf. 1 Cor 3:16), Peter compares the Christian community to a temple, a place for God to dwell on earth. Like the temple in Jerusalem at the time of Jesus, it is an unfinished structure. Christians are "being built into a spiritual house" as they come to Jesus for salvation (2:4). If it is true that 1 Peter is written after A.D. 70, it is likely that the recent destruction of the temple in Jerusalem lent special point and poignancy to Peter's metaphor. Christians can get along without a literal temple, Peter is saying, because they are themselves, through Jesus Christ, the temple and house of God. When Peter speaks later of judgment beginning "from the house of God," it is the same as beginning "from us" (4:17).

If the metaphor of "stones" is not an end in itself, neither is the metaphor of the temple as such. Christians are not a temple merely in order to *be* something, but to *do* something. They are a temple "for holy priesthood, to offer up spiritual sacrifices acceptable to God through Jesus Christ" (2:5). Peter's letter is the biblical basis for the time-honored Christian tradition of "the priesthood of all believers." This term in Protestant tradition has often been used to refer to the right of Christian believers to interpret Scripture according to the dictates of their individual consciences instead of being bound to the decisions of an institutional church or an authoritative clergy. But this is not Peter's meaning. There was in his time no "institutional church" or "authoritative clergy" to worry about. He himself provides for his readers an interpretation of certain biblical texts. Though he may have argued previously with the Jews about some of these texts, he assumes that his gentile Christian readers will accept his interpretations without question. This could be because he writes with the authority of an apostle, but more likely it is because he considered his interpretations a matter on which all right-minded Christians would naturally agree.

The "priesthood of believers" in 1 Peter, though based on Jewish Scripture, does not have to do with the interpretation of Scripture itself but with the offering of "spiritual sacrifices" (2:5). These sacrifices Peter defines both as Christian worship and Christian conduct. To offer them up to God is "to sound the praises of him who called you" (2:9) or simply to "glorify God" (4:16) or "revere Christ as Lord" (3:15) in word and action. They are the work not of a specially appointed clergy but of the whole people of God. Peter's words reinforce the words of Paul in Rom 12:1, urging that we present ourselves as "living sacrifices, holy and pleasing to God—which is your spiritual worship."

The designation of Christians as a "priesthood" is repeated in 1 Pet 2:9, where it is one designation among several. We are not only "the King's priesthood," but a "chosen race," a "holy nation," and a "people destined for vindication." Here Peter does not bother to cite a specific passage, but draws loosely on titles originally applied to Israel in Exod 19:6 and Isa 43:20–21. He does this without a trace of anti-Judaism or anti-Semitism, as if he were saying, "God has taken these titles of honor away from those wicked Jews and transferred them to us Christians." The Jews are not Peter's enemy. Christ the "living Stone" was "rejected by people generally" (2:4), not by the Jews in particular. Yet Peter does maintain that Gentile Christians now have a share in the identity, and consequently in the honor, that God conferred on the Jewish people centuries before. In their experience they have reenacted the experience of Israel: "Once you were no people, now you are God's people; once destitute of mercy, you have now received mercy" (2:10). Here he draws yet again on the language of Jewish Scripture, in this case the prophet Hosea (cf., e.g., Hos 1:9–10; 2:23). Just as Israel did not know God until he loved her and drew her to himself, so the Gentiles did not know

God until Jesus Christ called them through his messengers "out of darkness into his marvelous light." Though he makes no claim that they have displaced, or are displacing, Israel or the Jews as the people of God, Peter wants to assure his gentile Christian readers that Israel's history is their history and that Israel's hope of salvation is their hope too. Christian identity is obviously not the same as Jewish identity. For one thing it has no racial or ethnic base, and for another it is founded uniquely on the person and work of Jesus Christ. Yet to Peter our Christian identity is at least a corollary of Jewish identity. Both are founded on a common Scripture, and it is natural for Peter to draw on that Scripture to remind us of the privileges we share with Israel.

Though Peter draws generously on words from Isa 53 in describing the behavior of Jesus before his Passion and its implications (2:22, 24–25), he does not actually quote a passage of Scripture again until 3:10–12. Here he turns his attention to Ps 34:12–16, a text of central importance to his argument in the last half of the letter. As in 1:24 he introduces the citation with a simple conjunction (in this case "for") without the formal expression, "It is written." Again it scarcely matters whether or not his readers understand that he is quoting from a biblical text. The words speak for themselves. Peter has made the wisdom of the psalmist his own wisdom. The psalm is no longer an ancient Jewish text but a prophetic word of warning and promise to gentile Christians in Asia Minor and equally a word of warning and promise to Christians today. It blends gracefully with Peter's advice to all who read his letter to be "of one mind, sympathetic and full of brotherly affection, good-hearted and humble of mind," not to "return evil for evil, or insult for insult," but rather to "bless" those who curse them "so that you may inherit blessing" (3:8–9). In the psalm quotation Peter simply says it another way: they must "stop the tongue from evil and the lips from speaking deceit," they must "turn

The Past: Claiming a Heritage

from evil and do good," they must "seek peace and pursue it" (3:10–11). That is the way "to love life and see good days." The accompanying warning is that "the eyes of the Lord are on the just and his ears are open to their prayers, but the face of the Lord is against those who do evil" (v 12).

This quotation, placed roughly in the middle of 1 Peter, strikes several chords that are sounded again and again in the letter, both before and after. First, there is Peter's characteristic emphasis on sins of speech. He repeatedly warns his readers against "slanders" (2:1) and implies that they themselves have been, or will be, slandered and falsely accused of various crimes (2:12, 15; 3:16; 4:14–15). He sets forth the example of Jesus as one who "was insulted, but . . . would never insult in return" (2:23), and he explicitly warns Christians never to trade "insult for insult" with their enemies (3:9). Second, there is a characteristic accent on the sin of "deceit." In 1:22 Peter urges a brotherly affection that is "pure" (literally, "without hypocrisy") and in 2:2 an appetite for "spiritual milk," the very life of God given in mercy, as something "pure" (literally, "without deceit"). In 2:1, he tells us directly to get rid of "all malice," "all deceit," and "hypocrisies," while in 2:22 he describes Jesus as having "committed no sin, nor was deceit ever found on his lips." Third, the command to "turn from evil and do good" is a consistent theme throughout 1 Peter. Christians are repeatedly urged to "do good" in the face of slander (2:12, 13, 15, 20; 3:6, 16–17; 4:19) to the extent that "doing good" virtually defines what a Christian is. Fourth, the warning that "the eyes of the Lord are on the just" while "the face of the Lord is set against those who do evil" captures concisely the promise of vindication that dominates the latter half of the letter. If Christians "do good" and maintain a good conscience, those who slander and oppress them will be "put to shame" at the last day (3:16). Better to suffer now for doing good than on that day of retribution for doing evil! (3:17). On the day of God's judgment, Peter asks, "what will be the end of those who are disobedient to the gospel of God?" (4:17). Knowing this, Christians should follow the example of Jesus, who "never threatened [his enemies], but left them in the hands of him who judges justly" (2:23). In his last chapter (5:5), Peter finds the same principle of the vindication of the just in still another passage of Scripture: God "opposes the arrogant, but gives grace to the humble" (drawing on the words of Prov 3:34 and making them his own).

These examples demonstrate something of the uses Peter makes of the Jewish Scriptures. He does not read them in the heat of controversy or conflict but in much the same way any rabbi might do in instructing his Jewish flock. Yet Peter is not a rabbi (at least not in this letter). His "flock" is widely scattered, very far away, and not actually Jewish. Far more is going on in 1 Peter than simply the interpretation of Scripture. What is new is of course the life, teaching, death, and resurrection of Jesus Christ. Christianity is first of all a story, and Peter tells that story as convincingly as any New Testament writer. But Judaism had its stories too, and Peter saw the Christian story of Jesus (in part at least) in relation to the Jewish stories that preceded it. Some of these were written down in the Jewish Scriptures, some not. These stories, like the Scriptures themselves, Peter appropriates and adapts to Christian purposes for his gentile Christian readers. These are Christian stories, Peter insists, and their heroes and heroines provide for Christian believers in his own time a pattern for discipleship. Now, after centuries of familiarity with what Christians call the "Old Testament," many of us have been raised on these stories as well. Let's look at them anew through Peter's eyes.

The stories

Only three biblical figures are named in 1 Peter: Sarah, Abraham, and Noah. Beyond these, Peter is content to deal

The Past: Claiming a Heritage

in classes or types rather than individuals: the "holy wives" (of whom Sarah was one), the martyrs, the prophets, and the angels. He alludes very generally to a number of biblical stories on the assumption that his readers can fill in or imagine details for themselves. 1 Peter stands as evidence that many such stories were widely told and known even among gentile Christians in the first century. Two, however, Peter mentions specifically: the story of Sarah when she learned she was going to have a child and the story of Noah and the flood.

Sarah

The "story" in 1 Peter is nothing more than a passing allusion. Peter is urging wives to defer to their husbands' authority even when the husband is not a Christian. They are not to nag their husbands but win them over quietly, through purity of conduct and "a humble and quiet spirit" (3:1–4). Peter offers as an example "the holy wives who hoped in God" (v 5), probably the four matriarchs of Israel: Sarah, Rebecca, Rachel, and Leah (the wives of Abraham and Isaac, respectively, and the two wives of Jacob). Peter views the "holy wives" as Christians before the coming of Christ. They were "holy" even as Christians are called to be holy (cf. 1:15; 2:5, 9), and they "hoped in God" even as Christians do now through the resurrection of Jesus Christ (cf. 1:21).

Among the "holy wives" Peter singles out Sarah, who "obeyed Abraham when she called him 'Lord'" (3:6). That is all there is to the story! The reference is to the occasion when Sarah overheard the angel telling Abraham that she was to have a child. Sarah, according to the Greek translation of Gen 18:12, laughed and said, "This has never yet happened to me because my Lord is too old." The interest of the Genesis narrator, and of most Jewish commentators on the passage, centered on the problem of Sarah's irreverent laughter, but

Peter's attention is drawn instead to the single word "Lord." Amused and skeptical Sarah may have been, but at least she called Abraham her "lord"! On this one word Peter builds support for his advice to Christian wives in Asia Minor to defer to their husbands' authority. Just as in the case of the irony surrounding his own name and his personal history in the Gospel tradition, Peter "plays it straight." He ignores the irony in Sarah's story to make a sober and serious point about her relationship to Abraham.

Peter's use of the story is strange because any of his readers who were familiar with the story at all would have known that "Sarah laughed." The irony is still there, just beneath the surface, especially when we remember that the women to whom Peter was writing were not married to Abraham or anyone like him, but more likely than not to husbands "disobedient to the word" (3:1). Peter lets the irony in the story do its work without help from him, just as he did in 2:8 when citing a biblical text about "a stone for stumbling and a rock to trip over." His point is not that Christian wives in Asia Minor must literally call their husbands "Lord" (that title is everywhere else in 1 Peter reserved for Jesus Christ), still less that they must obey his every whim. Rather, Peter's argument is from the greater to the lesser: if in an ideal biblical relationship Sarah "obeyed" Abraham and called him "Lord" (even in her laughter), they should at least treat their husbands in a less-than-ideal relationship with deference and common respect. Though he does not say it, they might well have concluded that a little laughter would do no harm either! That he is still referring to less-than-ideal relationships is clear from his concluding words, "do good and let nothing frighten you" (3:6). The ideal of Christian marriage is attainable, Peter knows, only in situations where both husband and wife are believers, and even then it is not to be taken for granted.

Peter addresses the latter situation briefly in 3:7, but without invoking Abraham as an example to the men. Certainly there were aspects of Abraham's behavior toward Sarah that he would not have wanted his male readers to imitate! Instead, he works with the assumption that *all* Christians, not just the women, are "children of Sarah" (just as to Paul men and women alike are the "seed of Abraham," Gal 3:28–29). In 1 Peter *all* Christians are consistently called to "do good and let nothing frighten you" (cf. 2:15, 20; 3:13–14). All Christians are to have "that imperishable quality of a humble and quiet spirit" (3:4). There is nothing distinctly feminine about such characteristics. In other contexts they belong to Peter's description of the "imitation of Christ" (e.g., 2:21–23; cf. 3:9, 16; 5:5).

Peter's argument recalls that of Paul in Rom 4:16–25— except that Sarah and not Abraham is at the center. Sarah's story is ours as well through Jesus Christ, "delivered to death for our sins and raised to life for our justification" (Rom 4:25). We too have discovered that the God of Sarah, Rebecca, Rachel, and Leah is the God of Jesus who "raised him from the dead and gave him glory, so that your faith and hope might be in God" (1 Pet 1:21). In a society that offers us many celebrities and few heroes, the heroes and heroines of our biblical past (and of our Sunday school memories) are as valuable to us as they were to the wives and husbands of Asia Minor. The "holy wives" hoped for offspring in fulfillment of God's promises; we hope for eternal life through Jesus Christ our Lord, in fulfillment of the same eternal promises.

Noah

A strong interest among early Christians in the story of Noah and the flood is shown by their preservation of Jesus' saying, "As it was in the days of Noah, so it will be in the days of the Son of Man" (Luke 17:26 // Matt 24:37). Peter finds two significant parallels between Noah's day and his own. The first, which leads him into Noah's story, is the presence and reality of evil or "disobedient" spirits (1 Pet 3:19-20). The second is the experience of being "saved through water"— the waters of the flood in Noah's day, the waters of baptism in our own (3:21). A cluster of other parallels are implied but not quite stated: God was "waiting patiently" then, just as now; an ark was built for those being saved, just as Christians now "are being built into a spiritual house" (cf. 2:5); "few" were saved then, just as Christians are few in number in Peter's world (all these in 3:20). Peter sees Noah and his family, like Sarah and Abraham, as Christians who lived long before the coming of Christ.

Peter comes at the story of Noah rather obliquely. We do not usually think of evil spirits when we think of Noah, but Noah's story in Genesis is closely linked to an account of a strange incursion of evil into the world before the flood (Gen 6:1-8), implying that the flood followed as a judgment from God. Peter builds on an earlier three-part summary of the work of Jesus Christ that was probably already part of an early Christian creed:

1. Christ was "put to death in the flesh" (v 18)
2. He was "made alive in the Spirit" (v 18)
3. He "went to heaven" (v 22)

It was not unusual for the early Christians to summarize Christ's work in such concise formulas (cf., e.g., Rom 1:3, 4; 1 Tim 3:16), but what is unique to Peter is his accent on part 3, Christ's journey to heaven, and his explanation of its purpose. In the course of his journey, Christ "went and made proclamation to the spirits in refuge who were disobedient long ago . . . in the days of Noah," vv 19-20).

Who were these "disobedient spirits" and what did they have to do with Noah? Some have identified them as all the people who died in the flood, others with the disobedient angels or "sons of God" who took human wives, according to

Gen 6:2, 4, and so brought divine judgment on the ancient world. More likely they are the *offspring* of this evil union (Gen 6:4). In all likelihood Peter identifies them with the "spirits" mentioned in the gospels, the "unclean" or "evil" spirits Jesus encountered in his ministry and from which he delivered many who were sick or possessed. The victory over evil that began in Jesus' Galilean ministry is completed, according to Peter, after his resurrection.

Peter is drawing on more than just the story written in Genesis. He is indebted as well to Jewish traditions about the angels and their evil offspring preserved in certain popular apocalyptic works from the second century B.C. and later, above all *1* and *2 Enoch*. The mysterious offspring are called "Nephilim" in the Hebrew Bible ("miscarriages" according to some interpretations, "giants" according to others), but in Enoch quite explicitly "evil spirits" (cf. esp. *1 Enoch* 15.8–10). They are the link between Noah's day and the time of Jesus, for they were still active in the world to which Jesus came. They were not "in prison," as most translations would have it, for if they were, what would be Christ's proclamation to them? Would it be an announcement of their release? It is hard to imagine redemption through Christ releasing demonic forces into the world! Would it be an announcement of their subjection to Jesus Christ (3:22)? This is possible, yet it is hard to imagine what further "subjection" might mean in the case of spirits already "in prison"! More likely, the spirits are "in refuge," like the evil spirits inhabiting Babylon according to Rev 18:2. Christ's proclamation to them is that their safe havens are no longer safe. With all "angels and authorities and powers" (v 22), even they must now give way to Christ's authority. The subjection of these "disobedient spirits" is the measure of the universality of his rule. Peter's vision, no less than Paul's, is "that at the name of Jesus every knee should bow, in heaven and on earth and under the earth, and every tongue confess that Jesus Christ is Lord, to the glory of God the Father" (cf. Phil 2:10–11). The lordship of Jesus Christ so dramatically introduced in this unique passage guarantees to Christians a deliverance comparable to that of Noah and his family. Just as in the days of Noah, the people of God in Peter's day were being "saved through water"—in this case the water of baptism—from a world under judgment.

Such stories as these, whether in Genesis or in 1 Peter, leave many of us uneasy in the twentieth century. First, our scientific world-views tend to consign the "sons of God" and their offspring in Gen 6 to the realm of "myth," and with them the argument of this part of 1 Peter. Second, it is difficult for some to take seriously the notion that the times we live in are as evil and ripe for universal judgment as the days of Noah. Doesn't human progress mean anything? Hasn't technology made our lives easier and more productive? What could be wrong with that? Third, many evangelical Christians who are otherwise inclined to accept both Genesis and 1 Peter at face value are put off by Peter's notion that "baptism saves" (3:21). In light of all this, what do the stories of the disobedient spirits and of Noah have to say to us today?

With regard to myth, it is important not to assume that myths are necessarily fictions or untruths. Joseph Campbell has called myths "the world's dreams,"[1] and just as the God of the Bible is revealed often in dreams, there is no reason why God cannot reveal truth—even historical facts—in something identified by scholars as "myth." C. S. Lewis once wrote: "Just as God, in becoming Man, is 'emptied' of His glory, so the truth, when it comes down from the 'heaven' of myth to the 'earth' of history, undergoes a certain humiliation. Hence the New Testament is, and ought to be, more prosaic, in some ways less *splendid* than the Old. . . . Just as God is none the less God by being Man, so the Myth remains Myth even when it

The Past: Claiming a Heritage

becomes Fact."[2] We do well, therefore, to listen carefully to Peter's ancient stories, enter with wonder and imagination, like children, into the world they reveal to us, and try to hear what they are saying.

If we do this, we answer the second objection as well, for we are better prepared to accept the stubborn fact of evil in the world—no less in our world than in Noah's world, or Peter's. The real difficulty is not that the world is better or more peaceful than Peter portrays it, but just the opposite: that it is as bad as he portrays it, or worse. We are therefore compelled to ask, "How can this be if Christ has tamed all the evil spirits and put them under his sovereign control?" The answer is that Peter has here given us a "vision" of what Christ has accomplished in principle, not a sober account of what is already true in fact. If it were already true, there would be no more evil in the world. The Kingdom of God would have come. Nothing that Peter says here prevents him from reminding us near the end of his letter that "Your opponent, the devil, is on the move like a roaring lion ready to swallow [his prey]" (5:8). In 1 Peter, as in every book of the New Testament, the victory of Jesus Christ over the forces of evil is "already, but not yet."

Finally, how is it that baptism "saves"? Protestants especially have insisted that salvation is by faith alone, apart from any legal or ritual act we may perform, however valid or praiseworthy that act may be. Moreover, what do the comfortably heated waters of a baptismal tank or a few drops splashed on a baby's head by a priest have in common with the destructive flood that overwhelmed the entire world in Noah's day? Natural as such questions are, they reveal how bland and commonplace baptism has become in many of our churches. Yet Paul called baptism nothing less than a death and burial with Christ preparatory to rising with Christ to a new life (Rom 6:4). To Peter it suggests the flood, and the danger of death by drowning.[3] Noah and his family were not drowned, however; the waters of death sustained them in the ark and became the means of their salvation. Christians therefore do not "die" in baptism according to Peter. Baptism in 1 Peter is not death or burial, but resurrection (cf. v 21, "through the raising of Jesus Christ"). This means that baptism is not so much the putting off of the old life as the putting on of the new, not the "removal of the filth of the flesh" but an "appeal to God out of a good conscience." The "appeal" (or "pledge," as it is sometimes translated) is probably viewed here as a public appeal, identifying individuals once and for all as Christians in their respective cities or villages. Far from the badge of respectability it has become in the small towns of "Christian" America, baptism in Peter's time was a stigma in the eyes of many fellow citizens, an open invitation to slander and ridicule. To undergo baptism was to declare oneself a Christian publicly and to be ready to take the social consequences. To maintain a "good conscience" was to stand true to that public commitment no matter what the inconvenience or cost (3:16; cf. also 2:19, "out of a conscious commitment to God"). Because Peter would have assumed that those unwilling to take such a step were not genuine Christians, he has no hesitation in saying that baptism "now saves you" (v 21).

Baptism is for Peter the guarantee that a person has identified himself or herself irrevocably with Jesus Christ, even to suffering and death if it comes to that. It is consequently the guarantee of sharing with Christ in his resurrection and journey to heaven. In a context of hostility within the social order and the impending judgment of God, Peter understands "salvation" as rescue or deliverance, like the deliverance of Noah and his family from a world under judgment in their day. Because most of us do not live in such a crisis situation, we have spiritualized "salvation" into a kind of eternal inward blessedness, but the old stories told and retold—Noah's story and now Peter's—remind us that salvation is, first, survival and, second, vindication in the day when God judges the world. An old gospel song catches the spirit of 1 Peter better than most commentaries: "God gave Noah the rainbow sign: no more water but fire next time!" Peter has reached back into the Noah story for the imagery of water. Before he is finished, he will have something to say of fire as well (1 Pet 4:12, 17–19; cf. 1:6; also 2 Pet 3:5–7, 10–13).

The martyrs

The rest of the biblical stories in 1 Peter are left untold. Peter mentions none of their particulars. Instead, he refers to them as a class—what literary critics might call a genre—on the assumption that his readers can think of any number of specific examples to illustrate his point. The clearest case of this is 1 Pet 4:6, where he expands on a standard designation of God as "the One who stands ready to judge the living and the dead!" (v 5). This expression was a commonplace in Judaism: God would judge both the living and the dead at the end of the age on the basis of how faithfully they had kept his law. In a gentile Christian setting, however, more explanation was required. What mattered to the gentile Christians was the gospel of Jesus Christ, not the law, and their question would have been "How can God judge the dead if they have not heard the gospel of Jesus Christ?"

Peter's answer is not to explain the significance of the Jewish law as a basis for judgment, as Paul for example does in Rom 2. 1 Peter exhibits little or no interest in the law. Rather, he calls attention to those among the dead who *did* hear and believe the gospel of Jesus Christ—Christians before the coming of Christ, like Sarah and the "holy wives" and like Noah and his family. He states that "the gospel was proclaimed to those who are dead so that even though condemned in the flesh among people generally, they might live before God in the Spirit" (4:6). The point is that some now dead heard the gospel *while they were still alive* and paid the price of obedience to it, the same price that Christians may have to pay today. Yet God rewarded their obedience and faithfulness with the sure hope of resurrection, just as he will reward our obedience under similar circumstances.

What group does Peter have in mind here? What examples could he have cited? His brief reference should be read in the broadest possible terms, as all the righteous, all the faithful believers, whose stories are told in the Bible and Jewish tradition. His perspective is much like that of the Wisdom of Solomon, a Jewish work written in Greek some decades before 1 Peter and circulated widely among Jews and Christians alike:

> But the souls of the righteous are in the hands of God and no torment will ever touch them. In the eyes of the foolish they seemed to have died and their departure was thought to be affliction, and their going from us to be their destruction; but they are at peace. For though in the sight of men they were punished, their hope is full of immortality (Wisd Sol 3:1–4, RSV).

If we are looking for something more specific, many examples can be found in Heb 11, written possibly to Rome at a date close to the writing of 1 Peter from Rome. The author of Hebrews tells brief stories of many of the heroes and heroines of faith—Abel, Enoch, Noah, Abraham, Sarah, Isaac, Jacob, Joseph, Moses, Rahab—and, when he runs out of time, lists also Gideon, Barak, Samson, Jephthah, David, Samuel, and (as a group) the Jewish prophets and martyrs of Scripture and later tradition. Despite the long roll of names, many of the particulars of these stories are left to the readers' memory or imagination. Although conflict and suffering is not the major emphasis in Hebrews as it is in 1 Peter, the author does mention that Noah "condemned the world" when he built the ark (11:7), and that all the righteous up to Abraham were "foreigners and strangers on earth" (11:13), much like Peter and the Christians to whom he was writing (cf. 1 Pet 1:1; 2:11). Moses "chose to be mistreated along with the people of God rather than enjoy the pleasures of sin for a short time" and "regarded disgrace for the sake of Christ of greater value than the treasures of Egypt" (11:25, 27). Prophets and martyrs suffered all kinds of affliction and death for their faithfulness to the God of Israel (11:32–38). Martyred or not, they "all died in faith" (11:13) and for their faith received God's approval and the hope of resurrection (11:39).

These, in all likelihood, are "the dead" of whom Peter writes in 4:6. They received the "gospel" in their day just as surely as the Christians of Asia Minor had received it from the messengers of Jesus Christ in theirs (Heb 4:2: "For we also have had the gospel proclaimed to us just as they did"; cf. also v 6). The word of God is eternal, and always the same word, whether it is heard as the word of creation, the word of prophecy, or the explicit message of redemption through Jesus Christ (cf. again 1 Pet 1:23–25). In principle, the righteous of all ages are "gospel" people, and therefore Christians. Their common story, as Peter sees it, is our story as well. They believed, they suffered for their faith, they were faithful, they were vindicated. Peter has not the time, and feels no need, to spell out in detail their names and the circumstances of their struggles. Where the author of Hebrews cut his list of heroes short and left it to his readers to fill in the rest of the stories for themselves, Peter dispenses with the list altogether and contents himself with the general principle that God rescues his people from suffering and rewards their faithful obedience (cf. 2 Pet 2:9). Still, the passage opens for us the pages of the Old Testament to remind us that when we suffer because of our commitment to Jesus Christ, we are not alone but stand surrounded by a "great cloud of witnesses" (Heb 12:1) who have been this way before.

Peter uses biblical stories also to enhance our sense of wonder and mystery at the great salvation provided for us through Jesus Christ. This time the "heroes" are the prophets (1 Pet 1:10-12). As in the case of the martyrs, it is not a question of one particular incident involving Jewish prophets, but a whole class of incidents. Peter fastens our attention on an aspect of the prophets' role not often noticed. He reminds us that they not only gave out authoritative answers from God to the people of Israel—"Thus saith the Lord!"—but that they asked God many questions as well. There was much about the plan of salvation that they did *not* understand. Like Sarah and her husband, like Noah and his family, and like the "dead" who accepted the gospel in their lifetimes, these prophets were Christians long before the coming of Christ. They had the "spirit of Christ" among them, and with Christ's help they predicted "the sufferings intended for Christ and the glorious events that would follow" (1:11). Yet they themselves did not understand "the time and circumstances" of the events they were predicting. Therefore they made "careful and diligent inquiry" (1:10) and were told "that their ministry in regard to all this was not for their own benefit but for yours" (v 12). They were given a revelation, but the "revelation" was that for the time being nothing more would be revealed!

Peter may have in mind here such incidents as Daniel's prayer for the restoration of Jerusalem after seventy years of desolation, with the response from God that the desolation would be for seventy *weeks* of years (Dan 9). Or Daniel's question after a series of visions, "How long . . . until the end of these wonders?" and "What shall be the issue of these things?" (Dan 12:6, 8). Although certain precise time periods were mentioned, Daniel was finally told that "the words are shut up and sealed until the time of the end" (12:9). The visions were not for Daniel's own generation but for a much later time, and this is the point Peter wants to emphasize to his readers centuries later. The prophets prophesied "not for their own benefit, but for yours."

Another example is the prophet Habakkuk, who stood on his watchtower "to see what God will say to me" and was told, "the vision awaits its time. . . . If it seem slow, wait for it; it will surely come" (Hab 2:3). This was interpreted later by sectarian Jews to mean that "the final age shall be prolonged, and shall exceed all that the Prophets have said" (Qumran Pesher [Commentary] on Hab 7⁴). Most of the apocalyptic book known as *4 Ezra* consists of questions by "Ezra," the prophet who sees a series of visions from God, as to when and under what circumstances the visions he has seen will come to pass. He too is told that the visions are for a later indefinite time. These examples show that questions and uncertainties about ancient prophecies of the Messiah and the coming of God's Kingdom persisted in Judaism right up to Peter's day and beyond. It is to such uncertainties that Peter refers. He has just made the point that Jesus Christ, now invisible to human eyes, will soon be revealed with "praise, glory, and honor" to those who love him and believe in him. Then Christians will rejoice "with inexpressible and glorious delight" (1:7-8). The great salvation made possible by the work of Jesus Christ is beyond human comprehension or imagination. Even the prophets who predicted it did not understand it!

Almost as an afterthought, Peter suggests that even the angels, who normally explained things to inquiring prophets, were baffled by God's saving plan and still are. They desire to look down from heaven on what Christ has accomplished, but it is a mystery hidden even from their eyes! Yet this profound mystery "has been announced to you through those who brought you the gospel with the Holy Spirit sent from heaven" (1:12). Though Peter and the Christians of

Asia Minor still did not know what it was to meet Christ face to face, they shared in the good news of "the sufferings intended for Christ and the glorious events that would follow"—his death, his resurrection, his journey to heaven as Lord, and the hope of his appearing with glory and joy. The salvation of which the prophets had spoken was theirs in principle, even though they still awaited its visible and tangible realization. When we read 1 Peter, we stand where its first readers stood, and with them we read the Old Testament through Peter's eyes. There is much that we may not understand about the salvation Christ has won for us, but it begins with the "gospel" or "good news." The "gospel" in 1 Peter is the same gospel found in every other New Testament book, but Peter will explain it and develop its implications in a manner distinctly his own.

The Messiah

The Jewish heritage for Peter consisted of, first, the Scriptures, second, Jewish stories, and third, the Messiah. Of these the third was by far the most important, for it was the basis of the other two. Only the news that the Jewish Messiah had come in the person of Jesus gave these Gentiles a reason to read the Jewish Bible or listen to Jewish stories. As far as Jews were concerned, "Messiah" in Hebrew (the equivalent of "Christ" in Greek) meant "the anointed one," usually an anointed king or priest. Already in Paul's letters, however, and certainly by the time 1 Peter was written, "Christ" had become a name more than a title among Gentile Christians. Peter was an "apostle of Jesus Christ" (1:1), not "apostle of the Messiah Jesus." Christians were "sprinkled with the blood of Jesus Christ" (1:2), not with the blood of an anointed king. One can read Paul and 1 Peter without even remembering the Jewish origins of the designation "Christ." This is because the Christians had profoundly reinterpreted the Jewish notion of messiahship. Jesus is "Christ" more by virtue of his sufferings than his kingly power (cf. Luke 24:26, 46). The ancient prophets told of "sufferings intended for Christ" (1:11), as Peter demonstrates concretely from Isa 53:4–12 in 2:22 ("He committed no sin, neither was deceit ever found on his lips"), 2:24 ("He carried our sins"), and 2:25 ("By his wounding you have been healed" and "you were going astray like sheep"). Twice Peter introduces references to Christian suffering with the phrase, "for Christ also suffered" (2:21; 3:18). Twice he mentions "the sufferings of Christ" in relation to future glory (4:13; 5:1). Even when Christ is identified as the choice and precious "Stone" of biblical prophecy, he is "the stone which the builders rejected. . . . a stone for stumbling and a rock to trip over" (2:7). He is by no means the Messiah of popular expectation.

When Peter wants to emphasize the power and sovereignty of Jesus, he prefers the term "Lord" (e.g., 1:3), again following the precedent of Paul. In alluding to Isa 8:13 ("you must revere the Lord himself"), Peter identifies the "Lord" explicitly as "Christ"—meaning Jesus (1 Pet 3:15). Similarly in 1 Pet 1:25 and 2:3, the "Lord" referred to in certain Old Testament settings (i.e., the God of Israel) is assumed without discussion to be the same as Jesus Christ. The common early Christian interpretation of Ps 110:1 ("The Lord says to my lord, 'Sit at my right hand'") was that the Jewish "Messiah" or "Christ" was to be understood not merely as a descendant of King David but as David's "Lord" (David being the presumed speaker in the psalm). The term "Lord" was taken to be applicable both to God and to Jesus the Messiah. Once this happened, "Messiah" or "Christ" was no longer necessary as a title but came to be read, more often than not, as part of Jesus' name. Peter's acquaintance with this interpretation can be seen in his reference in 3:22 to Jesus "at the right hand of God." So closely is Jesus Christ identified with God that it is sometimes difficult to be sure whether Peter is referring to God or Jesus when he speaks of "the Lord" (in addition to 1:25 and 2:3, cf. also 2:13 and 3:12). Aside from Jesus and God, only Abraham is called "Lord" in 1 Peter (3:6), and in this instance (as we have seen) Sarah's laughter is almost audible behind the text if we listen for it!

1 Peter lays claim to a Jewish identity and a Jewish past on behalf of its gentile Christian readers. This heritage involved Jewish Scripture, Jewish stories, and the Jewish Messiah, but above all it involved the God of the Jewish people revealed decisively now to the rest of the world in Jesus of Nazareth. For a Gentile to accept God's "Messiah" or "Christ" (strange as that word was to a Greek or Roman) was to accept the God of Israel and to acknowledge this "foreign" deity as the only real God—a major step indeed! Following the precedent of most of Paul's letters, Peter identifies this God right at the outset in relation to Jesus as "the God and Father of our Lord Jesus Christ." It was "by raising Jesus Christ from the dead," Peter reminds these Gentiles, that the God of the Jews "gave us new birth" and "brought us to a living hope" (1:3). It was through Jesus, he reiterates, that "you are believers in God, who raised him from the dead and gave him glory, so that your faith and hope might be in God" (1:21). In short, they have come to share the status of the Jews as "a chosen race, the King's priesthood, a holy nation, a people destined for vindication" (2:9).

A marvelous blessing, or so it sounds as we read these words from the vantage point of the twentieth century! Yet in its own time it was by no means an unmixed blessing. What Greek or Roman in his right mind would want to take on the identity of the Jews, or share in the precarious situation the Jews faced in many cities and provinces of the Roman Empire? Anti-Semitism has a history far older than Christianity. Jews had gained certain political rights and a measure of social respect in parts of the empire, but the respect was hard won, long in coming, somewhat fragile, and in any case far from universal. Many ancient writers acknowledged the Jews' legitimacy because they were a real "nation" and a very ancient one at that, with well-defined laws and a very wise founder—Moses. Yet others distrusted them because of the strangeness of those same laws, particularly the ones about diet, circumcision, and the Sabbath. Why would any Gentile who was not born into the Jewish nation want to claim its identity? Those who did—at least those in view in 1 Peter—do not seem to have adopted these specific customs, yet they did claim, and Peter wants them to claim, the Jewish identity. This they did by virtue of their fascination with the Jewish Messiah and his God, and hence with the Jewish Scriptures and Jewish stories with their heroes and heroines.

For this, their fellow citizens in the provinces of Asia Minor where they lived probably viewed them with more suspicion than they viewed actual Jews, not less. Why were these people pretending to be Jews when they were not? They did not have the excuse that they were born into it nor that they literally belonged to this ancient and honorable nation. Therefore they did not have the political legitimacy that actual Jews had. Though Peter called them a "nation" (2:9), they were not a nation in the eyes either of the Romans or of the actual Jews. They were instead a voluntary association of Gentiles worshiping (from the Romans' viewpoint) a "strange god." Peter is writing at a time when neither the emperor nor his provincial governors knew exactly how to treat these Christians. They are not yet suffering persecution as a matter of official policy, but as we read 1 Peter we sense that all the makings of future persecution are present and that such things as social discrimination, hostile questioning, and slander were already common experiences. If the heritage of the past that Peter provides for Christians is a glorious one, their present is not so glorious. It is a time of aggravation and of the prospect of something far worse.

3 THE PRESENT: LIVING IN A HOSTILE SOCIETY

The 'fiery ordeal'

Peter's rhetoric about the social situation facing himself and his readers is most vivid in chapter 4 of his letter. "Dear friends," he begins, "don't be surprised at the fiery ordeal breaking out among you to put you to the test, as though something strange were happening to you" (4:12). His grim and urgent announcement is that it is now "time for the judgment to begin from the house of God, and if it is from us first, what will be the end of those who are disobedient to the gospel of God? And 'if the just person is barely saved, what will become of the godless and the sinner?'" (4:17–18). Peter's words have an apocalyptic ring to them, like Jesus' warning to the women of Jerusalem on his way to the cross: "Then they will begin to say to the mountains, 'Fall on us,' and to the hills, 'Cover us.' For if they do this when the wood is green, what will happen when it is dry?" (Luke 23:30–31). The apocalyptic tone continues in chapter 5: "Pay attention! Wake up! Your opponent, the devil, is on the move like a roaring lion ready to swallow [his prey]. Resist him, firm in faith, knowing that the same kinds of suffering are being accomplished in your brotherhood throughout the world" (5:8–9).

Many students of 1 Peter have suggested that this perspective does not govern the letter as a whole, but that in the course of composing it Peter either heard of or actually began to experience an outbreak of serious persecution at the hands of the Roman government. The relative calm of 1 Pet 1:1–4:11 is thereby contrasted with the alarm and fiery intensity of 4:12–5:14. The distinction, however, cannot be maintained. Already in chapter 1, Peter speaks in a similar vein. Even while promising his readers joy at the "salvation about to be revealed at the last day" (1:5–6a), Peter adds a sobering qualification: "—though now for a little you must suffer affliction in various ordeals. [You must suffer] so that the genuineness of your faith—a quality more precious than gold which, though perishable, is [also] tested by fire— may be found to result in praise, glory, and honor at the time when Jesus Christ is revealed" (1:6b–7). His rhetoric is somewhat more disjointed here than in chapters 4 and 5, but the point of it is much the same. The only difference is that a metaphor comparing Christian suffering with the process of refining gold in a smelter's furnace has given way in chapter 4 to the explicit term "fiery ordeal." To what is Peter referring? Does he mean that Christians were literally being burned at the stake, as Polycarp was in Asia Minor in the mid-second century?[1] If not, were they suffering physical violence, however administered? These questions must be answered by looking at 1 Peter as a whole, not by jumping to conclusions on the basis of a few highly rhetorical passages.

Even in the context of his reference to a "fiery ordeal," Peter goes on to explain more precisely what he has in mind. He speaks of "sharing in the sufferings of Christ" (4:13) and of suffering "for being a Christian" (4:16) or "when God requires it" (4:19). He also mentions the possibility of being "ridiculed for the name of Christ" and of the Spirit of God being "blasphemed" by those who do the ridiculing (4:14). Clearly, he does not concentrate on only one possible scenario—for example, a fiery or bloody persecution—but mentions a range of experiences or types of "suffering" that his readers might or might not have to undergo. It must be kept in mind that Peter is writing to the churches of Asia Minor from a thousand miles away and simply does not know all that has taken place among them, much less what might take place. The purpose of his rhetoric is to prepare them for an eventuality, not to fortify them in a known situation of bloodshed and violence.

Some have inferred that Peter is generalizing from a crisis that has broken out in his own community. His identification of the place from which he is writing as "Babylon" (5:12) lends some support to this theory, given the ancient significance of Babylon as the empire that oppressed the people of God by leading the Jews into captivity in 586 B.C. The designation "Babylon" is applied to the city of Rome in the Book of Revelation (cf. Rev 17:18), and it is natural to infer that Rome is meant in 1 Peter as well. The sinister depiction of "Babylon" in Rev 14:8; 16:19; 17:5-6, and throughout chapter 18 makes it easy to believe that Peter is writing from Rome and that the "fiery ordeal" of which he speaks is originating from that city—or even that the persecutions facing the readers of the letter are a matter of imperial policy. Many have suggested, in fact, that the sudden outbreak of persecution against Christians in the time of Nero (i.e., c. A.D. 64) took place even as Peter was preparing his letter to Asia Minor. Peter is said to have assumed—mistakenly, as it turned out—that the persecution would become worldwide, and he warned the Christians in Asia Minor accordingly. Others have supposed that 1 Peter was written in the second century, after persecution

The Present: Living in a Hostile Society

had become imperial policy, by someone other than the Apostle Peter.

Both theories read too much into the "fiery" language of chapter 4 and the reference to "Babylon" in 1 Pet 5:12. Though "Babylon" in that verse undoubtedly refers to Rome and stands as a clear self-testimony that Peter is writing from Rome, it carries with it none of the disgust and terror evident in "Babylon the Great, the mother of prostitutes and of the abominations of the earth, . . . the woman, drunk with the blood of the saints and the blood of the witnesses of Jesus" (Rev 17:5–6). "Babylon" here at the end of 1 Peter is simply the counterpart to "diaspora" at the beginning (1:1). It is the place of exile, the place where Christians, like the Jews of old, are "aliens and strangers" (2:11), living precariously in a culture that does not share their faith or their ethical commitments. Peter in Rome and his readers in Asia Minor are in the same boat, a counterculture in Roman society like the Jews but without the Jews' ancient credentials as a nation. 1 Peter is not addressed to a specific crisis, therefore, but speaks to situations faced by Christians everywhere and in every generation. Sometimes the hostility between the dominant culture and the people of God is readily apparent, and persecution looms almost visibly on the horizon. Sometimes the tensions are muted and the threats to faith more subtle, as in the "Christian" or "Judeo-Christian" cultures of the West. It is a difference in degree, not in kind. Biblical Christianity is never a "culture," but always, at least to some degree, a counterculture. American democracy, capitalism, European socialism, even some forms of communism may appropriate certain of its values (e.g., the doing of good, respect for others and especially those in authority, thrift, modesty, hard work, etc.), but other Christian traits (above all the love of one's enemies and a radical and exclusive commitment to the lordship of Jesus Christ) are apt to be unpopular in even the most "enlightened" societies. Hence the lasting relevance of 1 Peter.

If 1 Peter is not addressed to an actual present crisis, why the crisis language? Is Peter simply an alarmist, punctuating his legitimate concerns with a cry of "Fire!" and a dramatic summons to martyrdom? To some extent the urgency of his words echoes the urgency of the entire New Testament, from John the Baptist's "Repent, for the kingdom of heaven is near!" (Matt 3:2) to the concluding promise and prayer of the Book of Revelation, "'Yes, I am coming soon. . . .' Amen. Come, Lord Jesus" (Rev 22:20). With virtually every New Testament writer, Peter claims that "The end of all things is near" (1 Pet 4:7). At one level, the "fiery ordeal" mentioned in 4:12 is simply a corollary of this sense that the present order of things is coming to an end.

Another possible factor, however, is an awareness of the fate of the Jewish temple in Jerusalem. If the gentile Christian readers of 1 Peter are seen as "honorary Jews" laying claim to a Jewish heritage and a quasi-Jewish identity, then the temple at Jerusalem is their temple as well. Their reaction to the destruction of the temple by Roman armies in A.D. 70 would not have been to rejoice at the fulfillment of Jesus' prophecies (e.g., in Luke 21) or at the misfortune of "the wicked Jews" responsible for the death of Jesus, but rather to join with the Jews in mourning over the disappearance of the ancient and revered house of God.

The Gospel of Luke and the Book of Acts present the Jerusalem temple as the headquarters first of Jesus himself (e.g., Luke 2:41–50; 21:37–38) and later of his followers after his resurrection (e.g., Luke 24:53; Acts 2:46, 5:42). The temple's recent destruction by Roman armies could well have prompted the notion that Christians, even gentile Christians, were a new temple of God in a spiritual sense, "being built into a spiritual house for holy priesthood, to offer up spiritual sacrifices acceptable to God through Jesus Christ" (1 Pet 2:5). At the same time, the perception of that catastrophe as a judgment of God on the Jerusalem temple could have triggered Peter's urgent warning that it was "time for the judgment to begin from the house of God, and if it is from us first, what will be the end of those who are disobedient to the gospel of God?" (4:17). If God judged his ancient people by destroying their temple of stone and mortar, he could just as easily judge his new people, the spiritual temple built on Jesus Christ, the foundation stone. This time it would not be a matter of destruction but of putting his people to the test, so that their faith might emerge all the stronger (1:6–7). This judgment or "fiery ordeal" comes down finally to "various ordeals" (1:6), an accumulation of small harassments or aggravations of which Peter has heard but of which he has no specific or detailed knowledge.

Peter's conviction is that the God of Israel has a purpose in all these things. Positively, God's intent is to refine and purify his people that their faith may be shown to be genuine "at the time when Jesus Christ is revealed" (1:7). Negatively, God's intent is to begin the process of final judgment on the whole world. The effect of the "fire" of God's presence and power is to perfect and vindicate the righteous while destroying evil and those who do evil. The apocalyptic judgment of God starts in the particulars of countless small confrontations, whether in Rome or Asia Minor, between Christian faith and Greco-Roman culture, confrontations that often begin in the household but can spread quickly to arenas of public discourse such as the marketplace and the courts. Peter has no specific case histories to recite, yet much of his letter is taken up with general references to such confrontations and to the proper conduct of Christian believers in the face of slander, harassment, and aggravation. It is in this setting that Peter gives his answer to the question facing every serious Christian in every generation and every culture, "How should we then live?"

The troublemakers

The source of tension, whether in Peter's community or in the communities to which he is writing, remains unidentified through the first chapter of 1 Peter and into the second. In chapter 2, however, he reminds his readers that Jesus himself was "rejected by people generally" (2:4) and that to "unbelievers" Jesus is still "a stone for stumbling and a rock to trip over" (2:8). Peter's stern verdict on such people is that to such a fate "they were appointed" (2:9). Later it becomes clear that in mentioning "unbelievers" he is not referring merely to differences of opinion over theological matters. The disregard that these "unbelievers" have for Christ carries over to a disregard for those in Roman society who identify themselves as Christians. Peter refers vaguely to those who "accuse you of doing wrong" (2:12) or who "denounce your good conduct in Christ" (3:16). From the standpoint of the Christians they are troublemakers indeed.

It is not clear from Peter's words whether he has in mind mere gossip and slander or whether he knows of specific formal accusations being brought against Christians before ruling magistrates. Quite likely his language is purposely general in order to cover any eventuality. When he speaks of the possibility of a Christian suffering "as a murderer, or a thief, or criminal" (4:15), he seems to refer to actual trumped-up charges presented in court to discredit Christians and the Christian movement. It is fair to assume (especially in the wake of the brief outbreak of persecution in Rome under Nero) that he knew of cases where this had taken place. His counsel is that if such a thing should happen, believers must make absolutely sure there is no substance to any charges leveled against them. Their hands and their consciences must be clean so they can know in their hearts that they are suffering for their Christian faith and for no other reason (4:16).

It is unlikely, however, that formal charges in court are Peter's only, or even his principal, concern. Along with "murderer," "thief," and "criminal," he mentions "busybody" (4:15), a term more appropriate to the category of slander or name calling than to formal criminal charges. This is probably where his emphasis lies. Because of their high moral standards rooted in Judaism and in the teachings of Jesus, Christians may well have been denounced by fellow citizens as self-appointed guardians of public morality. Even pagan philosophers sometimes took such a role on themselves. Epictetus, a contemporary, speaks of Cynic philosophers who thought it their duty to "oversee" the conduct of others: "who is treating his wife well, and who ill; who quarrels; what household is stable, and what is not; making his rounds like a physician and feeling pulses" (*Dissertations* 3.22.72).

Such behavior did not make them popular. Plutarch describes the busybody who "creeps in, searching out with slanderous intent drunken revels and dances and all-night festivals" (*Moralia*, 517A). Christians and Jews frowned on such activities as well (cf. 1 Pet 4:3–4), and it is not difficult to see how they might have acquired a reputation for spoiling other people's fun! In some cases the reputation may even have been well deserved (cf. Paul's warnings in 1 Thess 4:11–12; 2 Thess 3:11; 1 Tim 5:13). Peter's intent is that Christians should bear testimony to their fellow citizens in such a way as to bring no reproach on the name of Jesus Christ. They should live according to their own faith and ethical standards while respecting the privacy of others. They should leave judgment and retribution to their God and refrain from passing their own judgments on the conduct of others. That way, any slanders brought against them will be just that, with no basis in fact. Then they will know they are suffering "for being a Christian" and for no other reason. They will have no need to be "ashamed" but will be able to "glorify God" freely and in good conscience (4:16).

Although 1 Peter is often read as a tract on physical suffering and martyrdom, it is striking that much of the abuse said to be facing Christians is verbal abuse. They can expect to be "accused" (2:12), "denounced" (3:16), and "ridiculed" (4:14). When Peter urges them to "put to silence the ignorance of the foolish" (2:15), he is referring to the silencing of foolish talk. It is largely a war of words, not of fire or sword or instruments of torture. Yet it is not for that reason a small thing. Because the Spirit of God rests on Christians when they are "ridiculed for the name of Christ," those who ridicule them are guilty of blasphemy of the Spirit (4:14; cf. vv 4–5).

In the world of the Bible, words matter. The ancients did not subscribe to the principle that "Sticks and stones can break my bones, but names can never hurt me." Words and names are weapons with enormous potential for either good or ill. For a Christian believer, words as well as actions must be brought under the lordship of Jesus Christ. Jesus himself was a victim of words before he was a victim of nails and a spear, yet he never used words for retaliation (2:22–23). Like him, Christians must not return "insult for insult, but on the contrary, bless—for this is what you are called to do, so that you may inherit blessing" (3:9). Peter commands his readers in the words of the psalmist to "stop the tongue from evil and the lips from speaking deceit" (3:10). They are to be silent when silence is appropriate and let their good deeds speak for them (3:1), yet when challenged they must be "ready to answer anyone who demands from you an accounting of the hope that is yours" (3:15). When they do speak, it must be with both kindness and integrity. They are to "get rid of all malice . . . and all deceit, as well as hypocrisies, jealousies, and slanders of every kind" (2:1). When they use words to worship God and minister to each other, whoever does the speaking must do so "as one bringing words from God" (4:11).

The Present: Living in a Hostile Society

Peter's accent on the crucial importance and utmost seriousness of the spoken word echoes the teaching of Jesus
himself (cf. Matt 12:35-37), and this accent is aptly echoed in
turn by a poem of Amos Niven Wilder:

Speak holy words—too many blasphemies,
Too many insolent and strident cries
And jeers and taunts and maledictions rise.

Speak faithful words—too many tongues that please,
And idle vows and disingenuous pleas,
And heartless and disheartening levities.

Speak quiet words—the constellations wait,
The mountains watch; the hour for man is late
Likewise to still his heart and supplicate.

Speak chastened words—for anguish is at hand,
Intolerable, that none can understand,
And writs of ill no mortal eye has scanned.

Speak gentle words—for fallen on the knives
These sentient hearts and these exceeded lives
Bleed till their pitying Advocate arrives.

Speak holy words—and O Thou tarrying Lord,
Leave not Thy cherished to the power of the sword;
Come with Thy hosts and rout the opprobrious horde.[2]

1 Peter preserves Judaism's ancient hope that God would
indeed "Come with His hosts and rout the opprobrious
horde." With the psalmist, Peter knows that "the eyes of the
Lord are on the just and his ears are open to their prayer, but
the face of the Lord is set against those who do evil" (3:12).
Those who now blaspheme God and the people of God will
one day "answer to the One who stands ready to judge the
living and the dead!" (4:5). Yet it is not the task of Christians

to threaten their adversaries or call down divine judgment on the troublemakers. The Maccabean martyrs in Jewish tradition did that, at least in their final agonies,[3] and Christ could have done it too, but he did not (2:23). For Christians to do so in the face of mere slander would only make their enemies' charges come true. They themselves would then have been the troublemakers. In principle, Christians are "free," Peter says, by virtue of being redeemed through Jesus Christ, but they must not make their spiritual freedom "an excuse to cause trouble" (2:16). The role of Christian believers is rather to love their enemies, returning good for evil and a blessing for a curse (3:9). This is the imitation of Christ (2:23).

Peter never quite brings himself to the point of saying "Love your enemies" in just those words. Already in Peter's time the words were too radical, too demanding. Yet the spirit of that command of Jesus (cf. esp. Luke 6:27–36) controls the ethical perspective of 1 Peter from beginning to end, even as it must control any ethic calling itself Christian in our generation or any other.

The state

Peter is always careful to distinguish the troublemakers who slandered Christians from those who administered justice in the Roman Empire, whether in Rome itself or in the provinces. He does this for two reasons: first, to blame the state for the harassment of Christians would only confirm suspicions that the followers of Christ were a subversive group in the empire, a threat to households and to the stability of the social order; second, Peter gives the impression that he is still genuinely confident and optimistic about Roman justice, even after the outbreak of persecution under Nero. He sees the emperor and his appointed magistrates as somehow representative of the entire Roman citizenry. All human beings (even the troublemakers!) deserve deference and respect simply because they are creatures of God (2:13). Preeminent and sovereign among them is the emperor, the "first citizen" of Rome, and next to him his appointed magistrates, whether in Rome or in the provinces. Peter wants his readers to demonstrate respect for their fellow citizens by respecting the emperor and his emissaries (cf. 1 Tim 2:1-2, "for all people—for kings and all who are in authority"; also Titus 3:1-2). The proper task of those in authority is "to punish wrongdoers and commend those who do good deeds" (2:14), and Peter implies every confidence that if Christians "do good" (2:12, 15), their good deeds will not go unrewarded. At the same time he implies that those who slander them unjustly will be punished as "wrongdoers," or, at the very least, put to silence (2:15).

Peter's vision in chapter 2 is that the Roman state will not turn out to be the enemy of the Christian movement but its protector, not out of favoritism but out of simple justice. He holds out the hope that even the troublemakers will experience a change of heart from observing the good works of Christians, and consequently come to "glorify God on the day of visitation" (2:12). Writing from the same Roman church that had received Paul's letter a decade or two earlier, Peter stands in a tradition established by Paul in Rom 13. He agrees with Paul that Christians should submit to imperial authority and that "rulers hold no terror for those who do right, but for those who do wrong" (Rom 13:1, 3). But where Paul wrote abstractly of "sovereign authorities," "the rulers," or "the authority," Peter refers directly and concretely to "the emperor" and to "magistrates . . . sent by him." More important, Peter stops short of saying that "the existing authorities are ordained by God" (Rom 13:1) or that the emperor is "God's servant" (Rom 13:4). The emperor represents the Roman people; he does not represent the God of Israel. Like every human being, he is God's creature and as such deserves honor and respect from

Christians "for the sake of the Lord" (2:13). That is as far as Peter is willing to go.

Within the New Testament, 1 Peter stands somewhere between the viewpoint of Paul, who saw Rome as a power established by God to rule over the Mediterranean world, and that of John in the Book of Revelation, who saw the Roman Empire as a horrible beast brought out of the sea by the devil to make war against the people of God (Rev 13:1–7). Clearly, Peter is closer to Paul than to the Book of Revelation, yet we have seen that he does not hesitate to call the city of Rome "Babylon" (5:12). He is also careful with his vocabulary. He tells his readers to "submit" or (better) "defer" to the emperor just as they should defer to any human being out of common respect. The notion of "obedience," however, he reserves for a believer's relationship to God or to Jesus Christ (cf., e.g., 1:2, 14, 22). If the two obligations should ever come into conflict, there is not the slightest doubt where the priority lies. Peter in this letter is the same Peter who speaks in Acts 5:29: "We must obey God rather than human beings."

Christian believers, set free from "the empty way of life that was your heritage" (1:17), are now "God's slaves" (2:16). Clearly then, responsibilities to God and each other take precedence over responsibilities to fellow citizens and to the emperor. Yet none of their obligations can be neglected. For the sake of survival and an effective mission for Christ in the Greco-Roman world, Peter strives for a balance: "show respect for everyone and love for the brotherhood, reverence toward God and respect for the emperor" (2:17). Again he is careful with his vocabulary. Jesus in Matthew and Luke said, "Love your enemy," while in John he said, "Love one another." Peter says, "love one another" but "respect everyone" (implicitly at least even the enemy). Honor is appropriate both to God and the emperor, but not the same honor. To Peter, "reverence" or "fear" is the honor due to God, while "respect" is appropriate to the emperor, as to every human being. Peter echoes the spirit if not the letter of Jesus' command, "Render to Caesar the things that are Caesar's, and to God the things that are God's" (Mark 12:17). He is more guarded than Paul in his endorsement of imperial authority, perhaps because he holds out just the shadow of a suspicion that a time might come when the emperor and his magistrates will *not* "punish wrongdoers and commend those who do good deeds" (2:14), but instead cause those who believe in Jesus Christ to "suffer for doing good" (2:20; 3:17; 4:19). That such suspicions were in fact justified is clear to us now from the Book of Revelation.

The household

The order and stability of the Roman state was built on the order and stability of households. The household was a kind of state in miniature. Yet the optimism with which Peter views the state does not carry over to the household to quite the same extent. The narrowing of his focus to the household (in 2:18–25 and 3:1–6) gives Peter the opportunity to explore possible circumstances in which Christians might have to "suffer for doing good." The reason is that not every slaveowner is as just or fair toward his household slaves as the emperor is (in Peter's eyes) toward his subjects, nor does every husband treat his wife with kindness or respect. Peter is interested specifically in the cruel slaveowner (2:18) and in the hostile or unbelieving husband (3:1). Despite his confidence that those who make trouble for Christian believers have no standing or decisive influence among the ruling authorities, he knows that in certain households the troublemakers are in charge, and it is to hard situations of this kind that he directs his primary attention. The oppressed Christian slave and the oppressed Christian wife serve as samples of what it means to live for Jesus Christ and suffer unjustly in hostile surroundings. Drawing on traditional catalogs of household duties known to ancient philosophers and moralists, Peter adapts these "household codes" to particular situations in which Christians faced the hostility of authority figures who did not share their faith.

Slaves and slaveowners

Christian slaves should "defer" to the authority of their owners, Peter writes, in the same way that all Christians should defer to the authority of the emperor and his magistrates. In the case of the emperor, the question does not come up, "What if a particular emperor is cruel and unjust?" Certainly the memory of Nero meant that this question, though unspoken, was very much in Peter's mind and in the minds of his readers. Yet it was not an expedient question to put in writing; better to assume that the emperor is always just and fair in the best tradition of Roman justice. The question is more easily dealt with in relation to households, where standards of justice and kindness varied enormously. Peter makes the point that the responsibility to be a good slave extends even to situations where the slaveowner is harsh and cruel (2:18). In Roman times, even a just slaveowner would have a slave beaten when the slave stole from him or mismanaged his property or mistreated other slaves, but Peter is more interested in "worst case scenarios," in which a slave does his best for the slaveowner, yet is cruelly mistreated (2:19–20). When this happens, it becomes a matter of "suffering for doing good," a major theme in 1 Peter as a whole. "To that purpose you have been called," Peter writes (2:21), and it is apparent from his words that he is not referring to a specific "calling" to be a slave, but to the destiny of all followers of Jesus Christ in a hostile world.

Jesus himself used the metaphor of slavery somewhat differently to make the same point: "'No servant is greater than his master.' If they persecuted me, they will persecute you also. If they obeyed my teaching, they will obey yours also. They will treat you this way because they do not know the One who sent me" (John 15:20–21; cf. Matt 10:24–25). Any Christian can expect to have to "suffer for doing good" under certain circumstances, just as Jesus did on his way to the cross and just as a slave does if he is unfortunate enough to belong to a cruel owner.

Peter is doing two things in this passage. First, he is giving real advice to real slaves on the assumption that there were slaves among his readers in the provinces of Asia Minor. Second, he uses the position of the slave in an unfriendly household as a metaphor for the position of every Christian believer in an unfriendly society—an unfriendly empire in fact, even though he has only good things to say about imperial authority. The fact that Peter does not also address slaveowners, even briefly, as Paul does in Col 4:1 and Eph 6:9, could suggest an awareness on his part that there were few if any Christian slaveowners in the congregations of Asia Minor. On the other hand, Colossians and Ephesians were also written to Asia Minor, and though these letters say much less to slaveowners than to slaves, they do complete the household code by at least including them. More likely, Peter omits any advice to slaveowners because they do not serve appropriately as a metaphor for the experience of suffering for doing good. He has just designated all Christian believers as "slaves of God" (2:16), and it is natural to follow this up with some reflection on what it means to belong to God, on the one hand, yet to have to cope with hostile human authorities, on the other. Despite the emphasis on "submission" or "deference" to human authorities, it is the obligation to God that controls—and if necessary supersedes—all other obligations. Deference to slaveowners must be "with deep reverence" (2:18), not reverence toward the owner but reverence toward God (cf. 2:17). Whenever a Christian slave—or any Christian—endures unjust affliction, he or she does so "out of a conscious commitment to God" (2:19), and when this happens Peter calls it "grace before God" (2:20). Only God makes it possible to "suffer for doing good," and God is the guarantor that such suffering will turn out to God's glory (cf. 4:16).

The relationship between slaves and slaveowners is not an easy one to reconstruct or understand in twentieth-century America. Peter's advice to Christian slaves is only partially applicable to Christian employees who work for unfair or demanding employers today. We now have all kinds of options and recourses that were not available to Christians in the Roman Empire. The value of the section lies not so much in its specific advice to slaves as in the setting it provides for Peter's profound notion of the imitation of Christ. Peter alone among the letter writers of the New Testament has developed the implications of the radical command of Jesus in the gospels, "Follow me." For Paul, as for the Gospel of John, the controlling imperative is to "believe" in Jesus Christ as Lord and Savior, so as to receive the salvation that Christ provided by his death on the cross. Peter, while not ignoring faith, has made a more considered attempt to do justice to the Synoptic Jesus and the invitation to follow in his footsteps and imitate his behavior. More of this in the next chapter.

Wives and husbands

If the world of slaves and slaveowners is rather remote, the world of marriage is still very much with us, even though marriage customs have changed over the years. Peter turns his attention to Christian wives in 3:1-6 and begins his advice with the now familiar command to "defer" to the one in authority—in the Roman world, the husband. Like the Apostle Paul, Peter endorses the dominant view of his time that authority in the household and the marriage relationship rests with the husband (cf. Col 3:18; Eph 5:22-24). He is not preoccupied with the "worst case scenario" to quite the same extent here as in the case of slaves, but he does focus largely on husbands who are "disobedient to the word"—that is, who do not believe in Jesus Christ. Mixed marriages were a problem for Christians in cases where the wife was a believer and the husband was not. It was less of a problem the other way around because the expectation and assumption of the culture was that a wife would naturally adopt her husband's religion. Hence Peter uses up six verses to address Christian wives and only one (v 7) to address Christian husbands.

Both Peter and Paul are often viewed from our twentieth-century perspective as traditionalists, even male chauvinists, with regard to sexuality and the marriage relationship, but it should be remembered that Peter is not telling Christian wives to "submit" or "defer" to their husbands' wishes in *every* respect. This would obviously mean adopting their husbands' religion (in most cases the Roman civic religion of the period) and renouncing their Christian faith. This was society's expectation. Peter is writing to women who must have been viewed already as highly insubordinate by many of their fellow citizens simply for remaining Christians. By Roman standards they were "liberated women" (perhaps dangerously so) and by no means the meekly submissive wives most husbands wanted. Their situation, therefore, was precarious. Peter's concern is that these women not aggravate an already tense situation by attempting to nag their husbands into the Kingdom of God. They must instead win their husbands over by letting their "reverent and pure conduct" do the talking for them (3:1-2).

This leads to the most explicit statement found anywhere in the New Testament on the subject of women's adornment (3:3-4). It is often the case in our culture that flamboyant dress and make-up is the hallmark of the "traditional" or "submissive" woman (e.g., the "Total Woman" of the early seventies). Feminists usually prefer more plain and modest apparel.

Quite the opposite was true in the Roman Empire, where lavish dress and adornment was a sign of liberation for female adherents of certain Eastern religious cults such as those of Artemis and Isis. These women were widely regarded as sexually provocative and therefore a threat to the social order and to the stability of households. Peter wants to make sure that Christian wives, "liberated" though they may be from their husbands' religion, are not perceived by their husbands—or anyone else—as religious troublemakers of this kind. His point is not simply that extravagant clothing is inappropriate for the Christian woman—though he undoubtedly believes this is the case. His point is rather that clothing and outward appearance—of *any* kind—is not what counts in the sight of God. What matters is not "your braided hair" or "the gold you put on" or "the clothes you wear" (3:3) but the real person underneath all the clothes, the braids, and the gold jewelry, "the person hidden in your heart, with that imperishable quality of a humble and quiet spirit." In God's sight this is the most lavish adornment of all (3:4).

Despite first impressions, Peter is no traditionalist. His affirmation of women as persons created in God's image and embodying the Spirit of God identifies him as a genuine Christian feminist. The "humble and quiet spirit" of which he writes is not the spirit of feminine submissiveness but a spirit that should characterize *every* Christian, male or female (cf. 3:8, 16, 5:5-6). It is in this connection that Peter introduces the example of the "holy wives" of Israel, and Sarah in particular. These women "hoped in God" (3:5) as every Christian now hopes in God (cf. 1:21). Christian wives are "children" of Sarah—and Abraham—for the same reason Christian men are "children" of Sarah and Abraham: because they have been redeemed through Jesus Christ. They are in all respects "co-heirs of the grace of life" (3:7).

Christian wives, like Christian slaves, are representative of all Christian believers in two principal ways: they are called to "defer" to those in authority over them (3:1, 5; cf. 2:18), and they are called to "do good" (3:1-2, 6; cf. 2:20). It is important to be clear about which of these responsibilities has the priority. Is the doing of good to be defined in terms of submission to authority, or is submission defined by the doing of good? What is it that Christians owe to those in authority? Do we "do good" by always doing what we are told, or by "doing the will of God" and being ready to face the consequences even in the face of ridicule and persecution. Peter's answer is that Christians owe the state, Christian slaves owe their owners, and Christian wives owe their unbelieving husbands deference and respect, but above all they owe them the gospel of Jesus Christ, "an accounting of the hope that is yours" (3:15), whether by word or example.

The goal of "good conduct" by Christians in Roman society—or any society—is that fellow citizens (even the troublemakers) "may, from observing your good works, glorify God on the day of visitation" (2:12). For wives, the goal is that their husbands might be won over "once they have observed your reverent and pure conduct" (3:2). Peter is far from certain that these things will happen. It is equally possible that troublemakers, cruel slaveowners, and unbelieving husbands will stubbornly "denounce your good conduct in Christ," and in such cases the goal is that they might be "put to shame" (3:16) either by the just intervention of Roman law (cf. 2:15) or (more likely) by the judgment of God. Christian wives, therefore, have nothing to fear if they "do good" (3:6), and the same is true of Christians generally: "So have no fear of them and don't be troubled" (3:13-14).

The "household duty codes" in 1 Peter are not the narrowly conformist tracts they may appear to be on a casual reading. The philosophy they express is not "Don't rock the boat," but "Don't rock the boat unnecessarily, or on your own whims." In some respects, the "boat" was already rocking more than was safe. So far as it is in their power, Peter wants his readers to be good and loyal subjects of the emperor, good and useful slaves if that is their lot, good and loving wives to their husbands. His word to us in every generation is to make sure that if we get in trouble with the state or our fellow citizens or employers or co-workers or with our spouses, it is because of our faith and not because of our personal stubbornness or selfishness. He sees no intrinsic virtue in suffering for suffering's sake, only in "suffering for doing good." Therein lies the imitation of Jesus Christ.

4   FROM PRESENT TO FUTURE

The threefold division of past, present, and future is a natural one, yet the nature of the material in 1 Peter requires a transitional step: Past/Present—From Present to Future—Future. The reason lies in a perception of time more characteristic of the ancient world than of our own. Bruce J. Malina has argued[1] that time has become for us in America and Northern Europe a very measurable thing and consequently very abstract. The present is but a tiny dot. Because our immediate needs for food and survival are met, we live for the future. What really counts is planning for that future, often a distant future, and to a lesser extent remembering the past. But in the ancient Mediterranean world, the world of the Bible, and in primitive societies even today, the present is a broad expanse of immediate experience and immediate needs encompassing in itself a remembered recent past and a "forthcoming" near future. The latter arises so directly and inevitably out of present experience that it is every bit as "real" as the present. Beyond this, the ancients had the notion of a more distant future in the sense in which we look to the future, but for them this future was not nearly so real. It was an "imaginary" future in distinction from the "forthcoming" future that they saw embedded in present experience.[2]

Malina's thesis is dramatically illustrated in 1 Peter. Malina remarks that the past was not important to the ancients except for certain Roman elite groups interested in family and the veneration of ancestors.[3] As we saw in chapter 3, however, the past was important also to the Jews and to Gentile Christians seeking an identity on the basis of Judaism's past. That identity, once established, helps explain the tensions and troubles of the present. Christians are objects of scorn and slander in the present because, like the Jews, they are "aliens and strangers" in Roman society. They have an "allotted time" in that society that they must spend in "reverent fear" of the God who redeemed them (1:17). They are called by God to live out their "remaining time in the flesh no longer for human impulses but to do the will of God" (4:3).

Peter's principal concern is with this troublesome present and with a "forthcoming" future implicit in the present situation. It is this "forthcoming" reality that constitutes the transition from present to future in 1 Peter. To understand the transition, it is necessary to understand Peter's vision of the Christian life both as an *imitatio Christi* (following Jesus Christ) and as a life lived in community (ministering in the family of God).

Following Jesus Christ

Unlike such heroes of biblical stories as Sarah, Noah, and the prophets or martyrs of Israel, Jesus Christ in 1 Peter is not a figure of the past but of the present, broadly understood. "Foreknown before the creation of the world," he has now "appeared in the last of the ages" (1:20). Though invisible

(1:8), Christ is part of the present just as surely as Christians are "now" the people of God (2:10), having "now" returned to their Shepherd (2:15) and "now" being saved in baptism through the power of his resurrection (3:21).

The way from the present into the future in 1 Peter is the way of Christian discipleship. Peter builds on the command of Jesus, "Follow me," directed to him and his brother Andrew at the beginning of Jesus' ministry in the Gospel of Mark (1:17) and echoed in the very last words of Jesus to him (or anyone else) after the resurrection according to the Gospel of John (21:22). In light of such personal references in the Gospel tradition, the strong accent on "following" Jesus in a New Testament letter attributed to Peter is not surprising. It is, however, distinctive in relation to the dominant emphasis in Paul's letters on "faith" and "believing." Faith or belief is a notion easily intellectualized. Although Paul did not so intend it, faith can be—and sometimes is—reduced merely to the holding of certain opinions about doctrine or the passive acceptance of the divine gift of salvation. Peter himself can speak of faith in God in Pauline terms (cf. 1:21), though he more commonly uses the word "obedience" for a person's initial acceptance of the Christian message (1:2, 22; cf. Paul in Rom 1:5; 15:18; 16:26). "Following" is the more dynamic term for it represents not merely an acceptance or a confession but an action. It is nothing less than the embarking on a journey with Christ to the cross and far beyond. To follow Jesus Christ is to participate both in his suffering and in his victory.

Sharing Christ's suffering

Discipleship in the gospels is frequently linked to Jesus' passion. "If anyone would come after me," Jesus announces, "let him deny himself and take up his cross and follow me. For whoever would save his life will lose it; and whoever loses his life for my sake and the gospel's will save it" (Mark 8:34–35). When Jesus tells Peter in the Gospel of John, "Where I am going you cannot follow now, but you will follow later," Peter is said to have replied, "Lord, why can't I follow you now? I will lay down my life for you" (John 13:36–37). Discipleship involves the prospect, or at least the possibility, of a violent death. The same is true in Peter's letter: "Christ also suffered for you, leaving you an example, that you might follow in his footsteps" (1 Pet 2:21). 1 Peter has often been described as a persecution document. If this means that bloody persecution was going on at the very moment 1 Peter was written, the term is certainly inaccurate. But if it means that persecution was part of the "forthcoming" future that Peter saw arising out of the present circumstances of Christians in the Roman Empire, then the term is appropriate.

The cross as example. What was it about the suffering and death of Jesus Christ that made it a fitting example to be imitated? Above all, it was undeserved or unjust suffering. Jesus suffered for doing good, not for doing evil, and in the course of his suffering he continued to do good: "He committed no sin, nor was deceit ever found on his lips. He was insulted, but he would never insult in return; when he suffered, he never threatened" (2:22–23). Jesus practiced nonretaliation in the face of both insult and injury, and Peter wants us to face the future in the same way: "Do not return evil for evil, or insult for insult, but on the contrary, bless—for this is what you are called to do" (3:9; cf. 2:21). Our "calling" as believers is to replicate in our lives the attitude and the behavior of Jesus Christ on his way to the cross. This means a clean break with sin and a firm commitment to "do good" in the sense of doing the will of God: "Now that Christ has suffered in the flesh, you too must arm yourselves with the same resolve—for he who suffered in the flesh is through with sin—so as to live out your remaining time in the flesh no longer for human impulses but to do the will of God" (4:1–2).

Peter is not bothered by the difficulty, obvious to us, that Christ was the sinless and divine Lord (1:19, 2:21) while we are mere fallible human beings. If Jesus is our example, Peter assumes, he is an example that can be imitated. This is not "perfectionism" as an abstract ideal but simply a practical, even naive, appeal to Christians to break with sin and "do good." Peter has no interest in debating theoretically whether or not such a break is possible. He merely says, "Do it." To the extent that we "share in the sufferings of Christ" in this way, he tells us to "be glad, so that when his glory is revealed you may rejoice all the more" (4:13).

The cross as redemption. The cross in 1 Peter is more than an example. It is also the instrument of our redemption. In this respect, Peter is in agreement with Paul and virtually every other New Testament writer. Almost at the beginning of his letter he identifies Christians as those "consecrated by the Spirit for obedience [i.e., acceptance of the gospel] and sprinkling with the blood of Jesus Christ" (1:2). He reminds his readers that they were "redeemed . . . not with perishable things such as silver or gold, but with precious blood, like that of a faultless and flawless lamb—the blood of Christ" (1:18-19). Having described Jesus' behavior in the face of unjust suffering (2:22-23), Peter concludes, "He himself carried our sins in his body to the cross, so that we, having parted with those sins, might live for what is right" (2:24). If Christ "suffered for you" in order to set an example (2:21), it is clear that he also "once suffered for sins, a just man on behalf of the unjust, that he might bring you to God" (3:18).

The metaphor of the lamb and the reference to the sprinkling of Christ's blood indicate that Peter regarded the death of Christ as a sacrifice (cf. Exod 12:5, 24:3-8; Isa 53:7). Much has been made of the theme of the Passover lamb in 1 Peter, to the extent even of suggesting that the whole letter is a Passover (or Easter) homily. In Greek the term *pascha*, an

From Present to Future

adaptation of the Hebrew *pesach,* "Passover," closely (but co-incidentally) resembles the verb for suffer (i.e., *pascho*), which is common in 1 Peter. But there is little evidence that Peter has in mind the Passover lamb in any exclusive sense. The lamb could be that, or it could be the lamb of Yom Kippur, the Day of Atonement, or it could be the lamb that Abraham told Isaac that God would provide according to Gen 22:8, or it could be the lamb to which the suffering servant of God is compared according to Isa 53:7. All that "lamb" or "sprinkled blood" suggests is sacrifice in a general sense, not a particular Jewish ritual or religious festival.

Like a sacrificial victim, Jesus Christ according to Peter was without fault or imperfection (1:19), a "just man" who "committed no sin" (2:22, 3:18). What exactly did his sacrifice accomplish? Christian theology commonly understands Christ's death as an "atonement," the removal of the guilt or penalty of sin in order to make forgiveness possible. But to Peter it is even more. Jesus Christ is not a passive sacrificial victim in Peter's theology of the cross, but an active sin-bearer and destroyer of our sins. If not quite the great high priest of the Epistle to the Hebrews (cf., e.g., Heb 2:17; 4:14-15; 5:5-6, 10; 6:20; 7:1-28), Jesus is nevertheless the one who "carried our sins in his body to the cross, so that we, *having parted with those sins,* might live for what is right" (2:24). He did not merely atone or compensate for our sins so that we can go on sinning and continually be forgiven. He quite literally did away with our sins, just as John the Baptist said he would do in the Gospel of John: "Look, the lamb of God who takes away the sin of the world!" (John 1:29; cf. 1 John 3:5: "But you know that he appeared so that he might take away our sins. And in him is no sin. No one who lives in him keeps on sinning").

This explains Peter's simple optimism about the possibility of Christians putting their sins behind them once and for all and doing only what is good for the rest of their lives (4:1-2).

The one who "suffered in the flesh" and is consequently "through with sin" (4:1) is probably to be understood as Jesus himself. To Peter, Jesus is "through with sin" not in the sense that he was once a sinner and gave it up (both 1:19 and 2:22 are against this), but in the sense that he finished dealing with sins when he carried them to the cross and left them there (cf. Heb 9:28). He suffered for sins "once" (3:18), and when they are gone, they are gone. Christians must "arm themselves with the same resolve" to be done with their sins forever (4:1-2).

Christian "realists" will object that this is an utterly unrealistic view of the Christian life. Centuries of Christian experience and the classic interpretations of Paul on the clash of the "old nature" and the "new" in the life of the believer cry out in protest against what Peter is saying. There is a "naiveté" in 1 Peter exceeded only by the naiveté of 1 John: "No one who lives in him keeps on sinning. No one who continues to sin has either seen him or known him" (1 John 3:6); "No one who is born of God will continue to sin, because God's seed remains in him; he cannot go on sinning, because he has been born of God" (1 John 3:9). Yet it is a naiveté that we need to hear. The kind of "realism" that begins by insisting on the inevitability of sin in the lives of believers is not going to make an impact for Christ by word or example in a hostile society. Peter knows this. He also knows that his readers have already made a decisive break with their past (1:18, 22-23; 4:3-4), and he dares to hope that their resistance to "the impulses that once drove you in your ignorance" (1:14) will continue (cf. 2:1, 11). He himself is realist enough to tell us to "remain constant in your love for each other, for love covers many sins" (4:8). He knows as well as the author of 1 John that "If we claim to be without sin, we deceive ourselves and the truth is not in us. If we confess our sins, he is faithful and just and will forgive us our sins and purify us from all unrighteousness" (1 John 1:8-9).

If there is a key to the realization of his command to put away sin and "do good," it rests not with individuals but with loving and forgiving Christian communities (see below, Ministering in the family of God).

1 Peter cuts through all the modern theological debates over whether the cross of Jesus Christ is simply an example of love and dedication or the divinely appointed means of redemption from sin. Traditionally, the so-called liberals have seen it as the former, while "conservatives" or "evangelicals" have resolutely insisted on the latter. In 1 Peter, without question, it is both. In 2:21-25 he moves naturally and easily from the cross as example (vv 21-23) to the cross as redemption (vv 24-25). The two aspects are not in tension in his mind, for to him each requires the other. Christian believers are able to put sin behind them and follow in the footsteps of Jesus Christ only because they have been redeemed through his blood. And redemption through the blood of Christ requires more than a passive acceptance of the saving benefits of his death. It requires in some sense an active participation in the death itself. To be a Christian believer is to follow Jesus Christ in the way of the cross.

Peter is not saying that his readers will necessarily be martyred, still less that they should seek martyrdom. His confidence rather is that their good deeds will "silence the ignorance of the foolish" (2:15). "Who then is going to harm you," he asks rhetorically, "if you are partisans for what is good?" (3:13). Yet he immediately adds that "*even if you should have to suffer* in the cause of justice you are blessed" (v 14). He knows that "suffering" takes many forms, beginning with social discrimination and verbal abuse, and that his readers are already suffering in various ways. Their "various ordeals" (1:6) are all part of the way of the cross. Peter wants, first, to prepare them for the possibility that things may get worse before they get better and, second, to direct their attention beyond even the cross to the victory of Jesus

Christ and the hope of vindication. The journey on which they have embarked does not end with the cross any more than Jesus' journey ended there. The future in 1 Peter is filled with hope and not despair.

Sharing Christ's victory

The risen Jesus in Luke's Gospel reminds two of his disciples of the biblical prophecies that the Messiah would "suffer these things and then enter his glory" (Luke 24:26). Peter too refers to "the sufferings intended for Christ and the glorious events that would follow" (1:11). He himself, like the elders of the congregations in Asia Minor, is a "witness to the sufferings of Christ and a sharer as well in the glory to be revealed" (5:1; cf. 4:13).

It might seem that the "glory to be revealed" belongs to the ultimate, or what Malina would call the "imaginary," future, a time of "inexpressible and glorious delight" (1:8) when the Christ who is now unseen will make himself visible. But the "glorious events" that were to follow Christ's suffering (1:11) belong at least in part to the broad expanse of the present and to a "forthcoming" future born of present circumstances. In connection with the "glory" of Christ, Malina's distinction between a remote, "imaginary" future and an immediate or "forthcoming" future begins to break down. Although some of Peter's language looks well beyond present experience, it is likely that Peter viewed the world in much the same way as Gerard Manley Hopkins, though with a different literary gift:

The world is charged with the grandeur of God
It will flame out, like shining from shook foil;
It gathers to a greatness, like the ooze of oil
Crushed. Why do men now not reck his rod?
Generations have trod, have trod, have trod;

And all is seared with trade; bleared, smeared with toil;
And wears man's smudge and shares man's smell; the soil
Is bare now, nor can foot feel, being shod.

And for all this, nature is never spent;
There lives the dearest freshness deep down things;
And though the last lights off the black West went
Oh, morning, and the brown brink eastward, springs—
Because the Holy Ghost over the bent
World broods with warm breast and with ah! bright wings.[4]

The "glorious events" of Christ in a "bent world" can be reconstructed and enumerated from many statements in 1 Peter. They must have included Jesus' resurrection (1:3; 3:21), which is explicitly defined as giving him "glory" (1:21); also his journey to heaven (3:22) and his enthronement at God's right hand, "with angels and authorities and powers in submission to him" (3:22). Last comes the visible "revelation" of Christ to his people with glory and salvation (1:5, 7, 13; 4:13; 5:4). Even this final glory is already "resting" on Christian believers through the power of the Spirit of God, in situations where they are "ridiculed for the name of Christ" (4:14; cf. Luke 12:11). Although it belongs to the future— even to Malina's "imaginary" future—the glory of Christ is also present in our darkest moments, brooding as Hopkins's "Holy Ghost over the bent / World broods with warm breast and with ah! bright wings."

"Glory" is left undefined in 1 Peter but always refers in some way to Christ's victory or vindication. "Glory" is vindication seen from the positive side; when vindication is viewed negatively the accent is rather on "shame" (2:6–7, 3:16) and on the judgment of God on Christ's adversaries. Christians who share in Christ's suffering are also called to share in his victory or vindication. This too is part of the journey. Peter sees two aspects to the victory of Jesus Christ: victory over death and victory over demons. They are the stages of his journey to heaven and to the "right hand of God" (3:22). Both were of decisive significance to Christians facing hostility in the Roman Empire, and both are of significance to us even after nineteen centuries.

Victory over death: the resurrection of Jesus. Almost at the beginning of his letter, Peter announces that God "in his great mercy gave us new birth by raising Jesus Christ from the dead" (1:3). By virtue of their rebirth, Christians have a "living hope, an indestructible, incorruptible, and unfading inheritance" (vv 3-4). Their lives are pointed toward the future and toward "a salvation about to be revealed at the last day" (v 5). The language of "being revealed," like the language of "glory," could suggest that salvation belongs to the ultimate or "imaginary" future, but Peter dispels such a notion by further describing salvation as "the outcome of your faith" (1:9). "Faith" is to be understood here not as "belief" but as "faithfulness" in the "various ordeals" of the present that results in "praise, glory, and honor at the time when Jesus Christ is revealed" (1:7). Salvation in 1 Peter does not come to us like a package sent from a distant planet but springs from present circumstances, however difficult, and from our obedient response to these circumstances. This becomes even clearer in chapter 2, where Peter, changing the metaphor, urges us to "grow up to salvation now that you have tasted that the Lord is good" (2:2-3).

Whether seen as the end of a growth process or as the end of a journey, "salvation" or "vindication" is something *toward which we are moving,* not something for which we are merely waiting. Christians are "a people destined for vindication" (2:9). The purpose of Christ's suffering was to "bring you to God" (3:18), not just to belief in God or the knowledge of God, but to God himself in heaven. Religious people commonly speak of "going to heaven" when they die, but it is surprising how seldom this expression occurs in the New

Testament. More surprising, the only person actually said to have "gone to heaven" in the New Testament is Jesus himself (1 Pet 3:22; cf. Acts 1:9-11). The only way to "go to heaven" in Peter's view is to follow Jesus there!

The difference between Peter's view and the popular "religious" view is that for Peter it is not a journey that begins at death. It is a journey that begins the moment a person undertakes to "follow" Jesus as a disciple. The Christian life in 1 Peter is a kind of pilgrimage, like the journey to the heavenly city in the Epistle to the Hebrews (cf. Heb 11:10, 14-16; 12:22; 13:14). Peter tells the gentile Christians of Asia Minor that "you were going astray like sheep, but you have turned now to the Shepherd and Guardian of your souls" (2:25). They are in the Shepherd's care, not as those placidly safe in the fold, but as those who will follow the Shepherd wherever he may lead. Their experience closely parallels that of Jesus' disciples in Mark's Gospel, to whom Jesus had said that the Scripture, "I will strike the shepherd, and the sheep will be scattered" (cf. Zech 13:7), was about to be fulfilled, adding that "*after I am risen*, I will lead you into Galilee" (Mark 14:27-28; cf. 16:7). The "missing link" in the context of 1 Pet 2:25 is any explicit reference to Jesus' resurrection. Jesus is "carrying our sins in his body to the cross" in v 24, and suddenly in v 25 he is very much alive again, welcoming Gentile converts as "the Shepherd and Guardian of your souls." The resurrection is clearly implied though not stated. Jesus has to be the *risen* Shepherd of the sheep (cf. Heb 13:20-21) in order for the disciple's journey even to begin.

In chapter 3 the resurrection of Jesus becomes explicit. Jesus is not only "put to death in the flesh" but is "made alive in the Spirit" (3:18). It is "in that state" (v 19)—as the risen Lord—that he makes his journey to heaven and leads his disciples there. In repentance and faith they experience the cleansing of conscience, "the removal of the filth of the flesh" (v 21; cf. 1:22; 2:1, 11). In baptism they make their appeal to God out of a cleansed conscience and are assured future salvation "through the raising of Jesus Christ" (v 21). If the justice of the Roman Empire fails them in times of ridicule and persecution, they have the far more secure hope of resurrection and eternal life.

Some scholars have drawn from Peter's emphasis on baptism the conclusion that the entire letter is based on a baptismal sermon or homily preached to new converts and later cast into the form of an epistle. Appeal is made to such phrases as "new birth" (1:3), "purified your souls" (1:22), "born anew" (1:23), and "newborn babies" (2:2), as well as the single explicit reference to baptism in 3:21. Such an elaborate theory is unlikely. It is more plausible that Peter, because he does not know his distant readers personally, approaches them on the basis of the one thing he knows they have in common with believers in his own congregation—they have believed in Christ and been baptized. Because baptism was the one experience that united all Christians whatever their location or external circumstances, it was natural and appropriate for Peter to appeal to baptism in a circular or diaspora letter intended for a large and distant group of congregations.

In Peter's view, baptism united Christian believers not only with Jesus Christ but with the righteous of Israel's past, like Noah and his family. With all the people of God, Christian believers now have the hope that "even though condemned in the flesh among people generally, they might live before God in the Spirit" (4:6). The principle that "God is not the God of the dead but of the living" (e.g., Mark 12:27) is here stated another way: God the Judge of both living and dead is the God of both because even the righteous dead will come alive through Jesus Christ (4:5-6). If believers have suffered for doing good, they will "inherit blessing" (3:9) for theirs is the way of "those who love life and see good days"

From Present to Future

(3:10). By the power of Jesus' resurrection, they are called to journey toward "his marvelous light" (2:10), or "his eternal glory—after you have suffered a little" (5:10a), and this secure hope assures them that God will "prepare, support, strengthen, and establish" them in the trials of the present" (5:10b). Like Jesus in the Gospel of John, Peter assures the faithful that they will not die, but that even if they die at the hands of their enemies they will live again (cf. John 11:25–26).

Victory over demons: the journey to heaven. The most distinctive contribution of 1 Peter to the Christian hope of vindication is the notion of Jesus' victory over demons and the demonic by virtue of his journey to heaven. In common with Paul and virtually every other early Christian writer, Peter proclaims that Jesus by his resurrection conquered death (cf. the words attributed to Peter at Pentecost in Acts 2:24–32). Peter alone, however, picks up the related thought that Jesus after his resurrection completed the work begun in his public ministry of subduing "unclean spirits" and setting free those who were demon-possessed (see, e.g., the accounts of Jesus' exorcisms in Mark 1:23–27; 5:1–20; and 9:14–29).

Without question, confrontation with demons and the demonic was a conspicuous feature of Jesus' ministry in Galilee. As a consequence of his ministry of exorcism, Jesus himself was accused of being demon-possessed and of casting out demons by the power of "Beelzebub, the ruler of demons" (e.g., Mark 3:22). "No one can enter a strong man's house," he countered, "unless he first bind the strong man; then indeed he may plunder his house" (Mark 3:27). Jesus' entire ministry can be regarded as the "binding of the strong man" (i.e., Beelzebub or Satan) and the "plundering of his house" (i.e., the freeing of his victims).

Modern Christians, even those who are quite conservative in their beliefs, do not find it easy to relate to such features of the Gospel story. In this respect they have ample precedent. Even the Gospel of John ignores the fact that Jesus was an exorcist—though it does cite Jesus as saying, "Now is the judgment of this world; now is the ruler of this world cast out" (John 12:31; cf. 14:30; 16:11). Although there are hints that Jesus' followers on occasion cast out demons after his resurrection (Acts 16:16–18), there is little evidence that the practice was encouraged (Acts 19:13–16). Paul does not mention "exorcisms" among the gifts of the Spirit in 1 Cor 12:8–11; if he endorsed them or knew of them at all, he must have classified them either under "gifts of healing" or "the working of miracles" (1 Cor 12:9–10). James seems to remember Gospel stories in which demons recognized the identity of Jesus (cf., e.g., Mark 1:24; 5:7), but he uses them only to illustrate a point: "Even the demons believe—and shudder" (James 2:19). So far as most of the New Testament is concerned, the story of Jesus and the "unclean spirits" is an unfinished story, and most twentieth-century theologians would be content to leave it that way.

1 Peter is a conspicuous exception. In connection with the traditional belief that Jesus Christ "was put to death in the flesh, but made alive in the Spirit" (3:18), the author adds that "in that state he *went* and made proclamation to the spirits in refuge who were disobedient long ago while God was waiting patiently in the days of Noah" (3:19–20a). This is his first explicit reference to Christ's "journey." Two verses later he concludes with Jesus "at the right hand of God, now that he has *gone to heaven*, with angels and authorities and powers in submission to him" (3:22). In both instances the journey is described in relation to certain supernatural beings, first "spirits," and then "angels and authorities and powers." The latter expression is universal in scope, like similar phrases in the letters of Paul (e.g., "every ruler and every authority and power" in 1 Cor 15:24, or "the rulers and authorities in the heavenly places" in Eph 3:10; see also Rom 8:38; Eph 1:21, 6:12; Phil 2:10; Col 1:16; 2:10, 15).

Like Paul and like the author of Hebrews, Peter picks up the language of certain biblical psalms to express his belief in the supremacy of Jesus Christ and the universality of his reign. Just as he uses the language of Ps 110:1 ("Sit at my right hand") for Christ's supremacy, so he adopts that of Ps 8:7 ("You have subjected all things under his feet") to describe Christ's universal lordship (cf. the explicit citation of Ps 8:7 to much the same effect in Heb 2:5–9 and by Paul in 1 Cor 15:27). Paul had used the two texts in a similar way in Eph 1:20, 22, where God is said to have made Christ "sit at his right hand in heavenly places" (Eph 1:20) and "subjected all things under his feet" (1:22). "All things" are defined in the context as "every ruler and authority and power and dominion and every name that is named, not only in this age but also in the age to come" (1:21). Without an actual citation of the text or even an explicit allusion, Peter makes the same point: Christ's rule is universal. Nothing and no one stands outside or beyond the reach of his sovereign rule and his righteous judgment.

The outer limits of Christ's rule are typified by "the spirits in refuge who were disobedient long ago . . . in the days of Noah" (3:19–20). These "disobedient spirits" of 1 Peter are best understood as corresponding to the demons or "unclean spirits" of the Gospel tradition. The reference to their disobedience, in fact, is Peter's explanation of the origin of demons. Like the authors of the Jewish apocalypse known as 1 Enoch, Peter views these "spirits" as offspring of the ungodly union described in Gen 6:1–4 between the "sons of God" and the "daughters of men": "But now the giants who are born from [the union of] spirits and the flesh shall be called evil spirits upon the earth. . . . They will become evil upon the earth and shall be called evil spirits" (1 Enoch 15.8–10). Peter links these spirits with Noah and the flood (3:20), apparently on the assumption that their disobedience "while God was waiting patiently" was what brought the floodwaters over the earth "in the days of Noah."

The spirits in 1 Peter are not in "prison" (see above, p. 22) but in "refuge," like the evil spirits inhabiting doomed Babylon according to Rev 18:2.[5] What would it mean, after all, to bring evil spirits into subjection to Christ if they were already "in prison"? Even Jesus, during his earthly ministry, had given the legion of "unclean spirits" a refuge, according to Mark 5:10–13, by allowing them to enter the bodies of two thousand pigs! The purpose of his proclamation in 1 Peter is not to release the spirits from prison—this would be anything but "good news"!—but to notify them that whatever refuges or safe havens they may have once enjoyed are no longer safe. Now at last they must prepare to yield to Christ's universal lordship (cf. 3:22).

The key term in this passage is not "in refuge" but "disobedient." These spirits were "disobedient" in Noah's time just as the troublemakers in the Roman Empire are said to be "disobedient" to the Gospel of Jesus Christ in Peter's day (cf. Peter's use of the same word in 2:8, 3:1, and 4:17). This is the reason they have a place in Peter's letter. 1 Pet 3:18–22 is not a digression but an integral part of his argument. The point is not that demons "symbolize" or represent the slanderers, the cruel slaveowners, or the unbelieving husbands who were causing trouble in various ways for the Christians of Asia Minor. Nor is it that these troublemakers are literally demon-possessed. The point is rather that if Christ could bring the notorious "disobedient spirits" of Noah's time under subjection, he can and will do the same to the human troublemakers who oppose the Christian gospel. No evil person or group, no social or political entity, however powerful it may be or however threatening to Christian believers, stands outside Christ's universal dominion. With "angels and authorities and powers in submission to him" (3:22), there is nothing for

From Present to Future

Christians to fear either in the household or in the market-place or in the courts (cf. 3:6, 13). Jesus Christ is Lord of all.

Peter is not interested in the phenomenon of "demon possession" in the strict sense, for he has broadened the definition of the demonic to include "disobedience" to God wherever it is found.[6] He leaves open the question whether the taming or subjection of disobedient powers is an aspect of redemption or of judgment. Those "disobeying the word" will "stumble," he says, just as they were "appointed" to do (2:8), and he asks rhetorically, "What will be the end of those who are disobedient to the gospel of God?" (4:17). Yet the possibility remains that husbands, for example, who are "disobedient to the word might be won over by their wives' conduct" (3:1). It is fair to assume that Peter leaves the door open in a similar way for troublemakers generally. It is possible *either* that those who "accuse you of doing wrong . . . may, from observing your good works, glorify God on the day of visitation" (2:12) *or* that, if they continue to "denounce your good conduct in Christ," they will end up being "put to shame" by divine judgment at the last day (3:16). Either way, Christians will be vindicated against their enemies just as certainly and decisively as Christ was vindicated in his confrontation with the "disobedient spirits" from the time of Noah.

Because of this, there is no reason to be contentious. Victory and vindication are assured. The proper stance of the Christian is "good conduct" (2:12; 3:1-2, 6; 3:16) after the example of Jesus himself (2:21-23). Respect and kindness even toward enemies and nonretaliation in the face of insult and injury (3:9) is an attitude that for Peter arises not out of weakness but out of strength and out of the conviction that through the resurrection and heavenly journey of Jesus Christ victory is assured. To say that victory is assured, however, is not the same as saying that victory is already won. Nothing in Jesus' proclamation to the "disobedient spirits" prevents Peter from sounding an alarm to his readers a chapter and a half later: "Pay attention! Wake up! Your opponent, the devil, is on the move like a roaring lion ready to swallow [his prey]. Resist him, firm in faith, knowing that the same kinds of suffering are being accomplished in your brotherhood throughout the world" (1 Pet 5:8-9).

This passage raises at least two questions. First, why is the devil not included with the "disobedient spirits" and all the "angels, authorities and powers" brought under subjection to Christ? Second, if the devil is "on the move like a roaring lion," how do we "resist" him while at the same time practicing nonresistance toward his human agents? The answer to the first question is that Christ's victory over the spirits by virtue of his journey to heaven is Peter's "vision." It is not something self-evident in everyday experience or in the state of the world as Peter perceived it—or as we perceive it, even with the "eyes of faith." Almost a century after Peter, an early Christian Gnostic was so carried away with the notion of Christ's victorious journey that he wrote,

"We suffered with him, and
we rose with him, and
we went to heaven with him"[7]

but Peter himself never goes go this far. Although Christ is victorious over the powers of evil *in principle*, his victory has yet to be realized in the "bent world," the world we actually live in, "seared with trade; bleared, smeared with toil."[8] In such a world it is by no means surprising that the devil is "on the move like a roaring lion, ready to swallow his prey." 1 Peter from beginning to end presupposes the devil's activity, even while attempting to put it within the larger perspective of the glory of God. He acknowledges that "now for a little you must suffer affliction" (1:6) and holds out the hope of eternal glory "after you have suffered a little" (5:10). The devil's rage and the suffering it brings are insignificant in comparison to Christ's victory (cf. Rom 8:18, 2 Cor 4:17), yet it is real, and Peter does not make the mistake of ignoring it.

The second question is, "How do we 'resist' the devil?" Peter's advice corresponds closely to that of James ("Resist the devil and he will flee from you," James 4:7) or to that of Paul in Ephesians: "Finally, be strong in the Lord and in the power of his might. Put on the full armor of God so that you may stand against the tricks of the devil. . . . Wear the full armor of God so as to resist in the evil day, and when you have done all this, to stand" (Eph 6:10–11, 13). In none of these passages is it possible to equate "resistance" to the devil with resistance to our human adversaries. Paul explicitly cautions that "our warfare is not against flesh and blood, but against the rulers, against the authorities, against the world powers of this darkness, against the spiritual forces of evil in heavenly places" (Eph 6:12). When Jesus warned his disciples "not to resist the evil one," his accompanying illustrations make it clear that he was referring not to the devil but to specific human enemies (Matt 5:39–42). The devil is to be resisted under all circumstances! Flannery O'Connor says of a character in one of her novels that he is "of the Devil because nothing in him resists the Devil. There's not much use to distinguish between them."[9]

Religious fanaticism comes into being as soon as we identify our enemies with the devil simplistically and without qualification. The fanatic sees evil only as something outside himself, never as something within himself. Peter does not make this mistake. Despite the parallel between the "disobedient spirits" and the enemies of Christianity in the Roman Empire, the devil in 1 Peter is "on the move like a roaring lion" not merely in the mischief wrought by these enemies but in the tendency of Christian believers themselves to deny or compromise their faith under pressure. To be "swallowed" by the devil is not to be slandered, harmed, or even killed by troublemakers or by the Roman authorities. It is rather to give up one's faith. No one is ever "swallowed" by the devil except by one's own consent. When Peter says, "Resist him, firm in faith" (5:9), the second phrase interprets the first. We resist the devil not by engaging in hostile action against anyone but by trusting God. Peter says, "Humble yourselves under the mighty hand of God, and when it is time he will lift you up. All your anxiety throw on him, for he cares about you" (5:6-7). James says, "Submit yourselves, therefore, to God. As you resist the devil, he will run from you" (James 4:7-8). The two commands amount to much the same thing for our relation to the devil—and to our enemies—is determined by our relationship to God. The only way to fight evil is to "do good." Peter's counsel echoes that of the Apostle Paul: "Do not be overcome with evil, but overcome evil with good" (Rom 12:21). When called upon to suffer for their faith and hope, Christian believers must never "be ashamed" but must "glorify God" and "entrust their lives to the faithful creator in the doing of good" (1 Pet 4:16, 19). This is how they follow Jesus Christ in his journey to heaven and his victory over the demonic world.

Ministering in the family of God

Not all of 1 Peter is occupied with the individual in relation to God, the devil, and human enemies. The Christian life is more than the achievement of individuals following Christ in the way of discipleship. It is a life lived in community. Peter's principal metaphor for this life together is that of the family. Besides "reverence" toward God" and "respect" for everyone, including the emperor, it is necessary to have "love for the brotherhood" (1 Pet 2:17). The entire letter, in fact, is written to the Christians of Asia Minor on behalf of "your brotherhood throughout the world" (5:9). The Christian community, whether local or worldwide, is a brother-and-sisterhood. The key to "facing outward" as witnesses for Christ to a hostile

From Present to Future

world is "facing inward" toward one another in love and mutual ministry. The very purpose of new life in Christ is "for pure brotherly affection" so that believers might "love one another unremittingly from the heart" (1:22).

To be sure, the family or household is not Peter's *only* image for the Christian community. A cluster of other images, mostly ethnic or political and all derived from a sense of identity with Israel and the Jews, can be found in chapter 2. Christian believers corporately are "a chosen race, the King's priesthood, a holy nation. . . . God's people" (2:9–10). Yet these metaphors do not illuminate the way in which Christians are to treat one another. They are directed toward the worship of God and witness for God in a hostile world ("to offer up spiritual sacrifices. . . . To sound the praises of him who called you out of darkness into his marvelous light," 2:5, 9), not toward the responsibility of love, mutual support, and mutual ministry *within* the worshiping congregation. For this aspect, Peter prefers the metaphor of the family or household, a sphere of life in which he has already shown interest in connection with the hostility and tension faced by Christian slaves (2:21–25) and Christian wives (3:1–6). Yet, for the most part in 1 Peter, the scene of Christian love in action is not the actual household but the worshiping congregation (4:7–11; 5:1–5). The household is more often a mission field, a place where belief confronts unbelief (3:1–6), than a place of prayer and mutual ministry based on a common faith.

Ministry in the household

Only very briefly, addressing Christian husbands in 3:7, does Peter afford himself a glimpse of what marriage can become when both husband and wife are believers. The brief reference is obviously not an adequate basis for a full-orbed view of Christian marriage, nor is it intended as such. Peter says nothing about children, as Paul does (however briefly) in Eph 6:1-4 and Col 3:20-21. He has no word about divorce and no advice for single parents. He is interested only in the way a Christian husband should treat his wife. Ordinarily in Roman society he could expect that his wife would become a Christian too if she was not one already, but he must be wise enough to leave the choice to her. He "must know how to live with a woman" whoever she may be and whatever her faith. He must show her "respect," or "honor," as "somebody weaker"—weaker physically, Peter assumes, but also weaker in terms of prestige and power in the society.

Weakness does not normally bring a person "respect" or "honor" in any culture. Quite the contrary. We would have expected him to say, "Respect your wife *despite* her weakness," not *because* of it. Peter, however, is already presupposing a distinctly Christian vision of weakness and power, in which God honors and exalts those who are—or make themselves—"last" or "least" in the eyes of the world (cf., e.g., Jesus' teaching in Mark 9:33-37, 10:42-45; Matt 18:1-4; also Paul in 1 Cor 12:22-24). What is true in the sight of God must be true as well among the people of God. The "respect" and "honor" a woman lacked in Roman society could be and should be hers from her Christian husband. Obviously, Peter could just as easily have said "Husbands, love your wives," as Paul did in Eph 5:25 and Col 3:19, but he does not. He limits himself to the more formal and impersonal term, "respect" or "honor," possibly because he is looking more at the social roles in marriage than at the personal relationships between a husband and a wife. "Love" (Greek, *agapao*) is a verb that Peter reserves for *all* Christians in relation to *all* other Christians—viewed as one's "brothers" and "sisters"—in the Christian community. He never uses it in relation to one's "neighbors" in Roman society or one's "enemies," nor does he use it for *specific* relationships such as that of a wife to her husband or a husband to his wife. "Love" among Christians is for "one another" (1:22, 4:8) without distinction or discrimination.

The household in the Roman Empire was an institution intended to support and undergird the authority of the state and the emperor. Households were viewed by Roman philosophers as the very fabric of the empire, just as today the strength of families is widely viewed as the key to the strength of America. Peter, however, saw the family potentially, if not actually, as a safeguard against the abuses and shortcomings that he saw as all too prevalent in the empire. If to Roman philosophers it was a kind of empire in miniature, Peter wanted it to function as a church in miniature. He knew it did not always do so—often because the husband was not a believer—yet the family becomes his model for the worshiping and ministering congregation. When both husband and wife are Christian believers, they are "co-heirs of the grace of life," and Peter is confident that their "prayers will not be hindered" (3:7b). He does not labor the point, but one suspects Peter might have agreed with Clement of Alexandria in the third century, who, in interpreting Matt 18:20, asked, "But who are the two or three gathered in the name of Christ in whose midst the Lord is? Does he not by the 'three' mean husband, wife and child?"[10]

Peter expresses himself somewhat differently, but his point is much the same. It is not the presence of the Holy Spirit or the risen Lord that interests him, but "grace," specifically the "grace of life" that belongs to the future, yet decisively shapes Christian households and congregations even in the present. Peter designates Christian husbands and their wives as "co-heirs" of this grace prophesied long ago by the prophets (1:10) and still waiting "to be brought to you when Jesus Christ is revealed" (1:13). Peter comes back again and again to this "grace" operative in advance in varied forms in the ministry and worship of the congregations to which he writes (4:10, 5:5), and even in his own ministry of letter writing to those same congregations (5:12).

Ministry in the congregation

The proper sphere of ministry in 1 Peter, as in the New Testament generally, is the "church" or worshiping congregation. Although the actual word "church" (Greek, *ekklesia*) never occurs in this letter, the ministry of Christian believers to one another in worship assemblies is described twice, in 1 Pet 4:7–11 and 5:1–5. The difference between the two passages is that in the first Peter assumes the equality of all members in the congregation, with each ministering to the others on the basis of the spiritual gifts he or she has received (4:7–11; cf. Paul in 1 Cor 12:4–11; 14:26–33; and Rom 12:3–8), while in the second Peter distinguishes clearly between "elders" and "You . . . who are younger," addressing each in turn but emphasizing throughout the responsibility of the "elders" to exercise leadership over the congregation (5:1–5; cf. 1 Tim 3:1–13; 5:17–22). It is natural to ask how Peter is able to reconcile in his mind these two very different perspectives on Christian ministry, but this question can be answered only after each has been examined in its own context.

Mutual ministries. Peter's depiction of Christian ministry in 4:7–11 is governed by the firm conviction that "The end of all things is near" (v 7)—the same conviction that governs everything he writes. If individual discipleship is a journey in the footsteps of Jesus Christ toward heaven and the future, Christian life in community is a life shaped by an awareness that God's future is breaking into the present. Only by looking together toward that future is it possible to work effectively as the people of God.

Peter attempts to build community in these distant congregations not "horizontally," by turning the eyes of Christians toward each other, but "vertically," by fixing their attention on God and what God intends. When he tells them to "Prepare yourselves mentally, therefore, and attend to prayers" (4:7b), he is simply reiterating what he had said in chapter 1: "Gird yourselves for action, therefore, in your mind, and with full attention set your hope on the grace to be brought to you when Jesus Christ is revealed" (1:13). Peter would have appreciated Augustine's comparison of two Christian believers united in the love of Christ with two eyes in a single body. Like a person's eyes, they are separate and do not look at each other, yet are focused together on God as the object of their common vision. "Together they meet in one object," Augustine wrote, "together they are directed to one object; their aim is one, their places diverse."[11] What is true for two people is just as true for whole communities of believers. They will find unity not by self-consciously trying to "relate" to each other, but by looking together in prayer and hope toward the God who called them and for whom they live.

Within this community, Peter knows no hierarchy. All Christian believers are to have love "for each other" (4:8), practice hospitality "toward one another" (4:9), and be ministers "to each other" (4:10). Love is the dominant command here, as everywhere else in the New Testament, and love is focused in 1 Peter specifically on those who share a common faith in God through Jesus Christ (cf. the perspective of John's Gospel and epistles, as, e.g., in John 13:34; 15:12; 1 John 4:7, 11, 21; 2 John 5). Mutual hospitality and ministry are but the concrete expressions of mutual love. Before love can lead to ministry, however, or to hospitality toward those who minister, it must lead to mutual forgiveness. The first thing Peter says about love is that it "covers many sins" (v 8b). He is not referring to the illegitimate concealment of wrongdoing but to forgiveness in the context of a community of believers. Peter is recognizing and emphasizing the social character of most of the sins that Christians commit. What we do ordinarily affects those we love, for good or ill—both our actual family members and the members of our new family in Christ. Sins committed in—or against—the community of faith must find forgiveness and cleansing in that same community. Internal or individual "sins of the heart" do not come into the picture here. Only in a communal setting of mutual love does Peter envision a realization of the ideal expressed elsewhere in his letter of "having parted with . . . sins" (2:24) or being "through with sin" (4:1) as a result of the death of Jesus Christ.

Hospitality was a virtue of great importance in the Roman church. Both Paul (Rom 12:13) and the author of Hebrews (Heb 13:2) had urged the Roman Christians to practice it, while Clement, a Roman elder near the end of the first century, held up Abraham, Lot, and Rahab as classic biblical examples of this virtue to the church at Corinth (1 Clem. 10–12). Peter too lists mutual hospitality (4:9) as an appropriate expression of Christian love. He shows little evidence of firsthand knowledge of the Asian congregations to which he writes, but he does know they are widely scattered, probably not affluent, and therefore dependent on the generosity and good will of their members.

Hospitality among Christians in the first century was not a matter of courtesy or etiquette but of survival. Within particular congregations, it was necessary that some be willing to open their homes as house churches (cf. Rom 16:5, 1 Cor 16:19, and in Asia Minor Col 4:15 and Phlm 2). Among the various congregations, it was necessary that itinerant prophets and teachers, as well as messengers from one congregation to another, be welcomed, fed, and lodged (cf. 3 John 5–8; also the extensive discussion in the second century in the Didache, chs 11–13). Knowing that the well-being of the Christian movement in Asia Minor, and of the individual congregations that comprised it, depended on hospitality, Peter singles out this virtue as the simplest and most basic expression of mutual love. Because he also knew that hospitality was sometimes taken for granted or abused by those receiving it, he adds that it should be given "without complaining." For himself, his unstated hope is that the hospitality of his readers might include the warm reception of his letter and of Silvanus, the messenger who will deliver it (5:12). For the present, however, he leaves himself out of it and is content to urge on his readers hospitality "toward one another" in general rather than specific or personal terms. It is a responsibility incumbent on all, a ministry in which everyone participates.

Other ministries depend on "spiritual gifts" (Greek, *charisma*, 4:10). Peter assumes that the congregations to which he is writing are "charismatic" in much the same sense as the congregations established by Paul (e.g., at Thessalonica and Corinth). Yet he does not attempt to list a whole range of "gifts of the Spirit," as Paul does in 1 Cor 12. He does not even call them "gifts of the Spirit" or mention the Holy Spirit at all in this connection. Peter may have taken his cue from Paul himself, who in a more simplified list of gifts in his letter to the congregations at Rome had also omitted any reference to the Spirit (cf. Rom 12:6–8). It cannot be inferred, therefore, that Peter saw no link between the Spirit and the work of ministry in the local congregation. If the Spirit was at work in the ancient prophets (1:11), in the evangelization and consecration of new converts throughout the Roman Empire (1:2, 12), and in the testimony of Christians to those who ridiculed and harassed them (4:14), it would be natural to find the Spirit introduced in connection with the ministry of believers to one another. A possible reason why Peter does not mention the Spirit explicitly is that he does not view the Spirit as an independent entity in quite the way Paul does, but more as a pointer to something (or Someone) else. The Spirit in 1 Peter is the "spirit of Christ" (1:11) or "the Spirit of God" or of God's glory (4:14). For the translator, it is even difficult to know when the term should be capitalized and when not.

In the present passage, "God" and not "Spirit" is said to be the source and power behind all the varied ministries in the Christian congregation, and "God" is also the one to whom all ministries are accountable. Such expressions as "God's diversified grace" (4:10), "words from God," "strength that God provides," and "so that in all things God may be glorified" (4:11) contribute to a remarkable God-centeredness in these brief directives of Peter to a typical congregation. God is above all the author of "grace" (Greek, *charis*). The future "grace to be brought to you when Jesus Christ is revealed" (1:13), the grace of which Christian women and men are "coheirs" (3:7), is here seen as "diversified," operating in advance in the words and deeds with which Christian believers minister to one another. It is at once the object of future hope and the core of present experience and practice.

Peter makes no attempt to classify the varied gifts of God to the people of God. He is content to divide them into gifts of *speaking* ("as . . . words from God") and of *serving* ("out of strength that God provides"). Under the first heading come the gifts of tongues, prophecy, exhortation, and teaching, while the second might include healing, helping the poor, administration, settling disputes, and supervising corporate worship. At the end of his letter (5:12) Peter sees himself and the letter he has just written within this framework of mutual ministry. 1 Peter itself is described as "true grace from God." Peter asks to be accepted by his readers as part of their extended congregation. He too is a "good manager of God's diversified grace," and his written words, like words spoken in their worship assemblies, cry out to be received and welcomed as "words from God." His expectation was that his letter would be actually read aloud in their congregations assembled for worship and mutual ministry (cf. Paul's expectation according to Col 4:16). The concluding salutation in 1 Pet 5:12–14 could have appropriately followed the summary of ministries in 4:7–11 in a smooth and natural sequence. The summary ends with a doxology (v 11b), as if Peter is about to bring his letter to a conclusion. This is not the case, however, in the letter as it stands. Peter has more to say on the subject of ministry in the family of God, and he will say it in the intervening chapter.

The ministry of elders. The address, "Dear friends," in 4:12 introduces a new major section of 1 Peter (4:12–5:11) with its own perspective on ministry (5:1–5) and its own doxology at the end (5:10–11). Our expectation is that he is going to say, "Dear friends, I appeal to you," just as he had done two chapters earlier (in 2:11). Instead, he postpones the "appeal" until 5:1, and when it comes it is an appeal not to all believers indiscriminately but to "any elders among you." In mentioning "elders," Peter discloses an aspect of Christian ministry which he had not even hinted at in 4:7–11. Elders in the ancient church seem to have been the first converts to Christianity in any given city or geographical area. In some instances they were given positions of responsibility in the congregation on the basis of their seniority. Although Paul mentions and gives credit to Epaenetus, "the first convert in Asia for Christ" (Rom 16:5), and to the household of Stephanas as "the first converts in Achaia" (or Greece), he nowhere refers to "elders" in his earlier letters. Only in the Book of Acts (14:23; 20:17) and in the Pastoral letters (1 Tim 5:1–2, 17, 19; Tit 1:5) are elders explicitly associated with churches established by Paul (for other churches, cf. James 5:14).

Peter's apparent assumption in writing 1 Peter is that some of the distant congregations that will read his letter are ruled by elders and some are not. He therefore includes both an "all-purpose" section on mutual ministry (4:7–11) and a section geared specifically toward congregations in which pastoral responsibility rests with a group of elders. The principles of love, hospitality, and ministry expressed in 4:7–11 are applicable everywhere in light of the conviction that "the end of all things is near" (4:7), but in congregations ruled by elders the demands of the time place a special burden on them. It is not a matter of hierarchy but of de facto responsibility. In describing the "fiery ordeal" facing the people of God, Peter states that it is "time for the judgment to begin from the house of God" (4:17). His language draws on the imagery of Ezek 9:6, where the judgment of God began not only from the "sanctuary," or temple of God in Jerusalem, but "from the men who were elders, inside the house." This imagery, suggested to him perhaps by the recent destruction of Jerusalem and its temple by Roman armies, provides the occasion and opportunity to focus on Christian "elders" and their responsibility in a comparable crisis. 1 Pet 4:12–19 thus serves as the indispensable setting for Peter's directives to "any elders among you" in 5:1–5.

Peter writes to them as their "fellow elder" (5:1), perhaps because he was himself an elder of the Roman church but more likely as one of the founders of the Christian movement generally (cf. "apostle of Jesus Christ" in 1 Pet 1:1). As an authority figure in the movement, his concern is not to assert that authority *over* the elders of Asia Minor but to establish common ground *with* them. His approach is reminiscent of John's approach to his readers in Rev 1:9 as "your brother and companion in the suffering and kingdom and patient endurance that are ours in Jesus." If every Christian believer is a "witness to the sufferings of Christ" and a "sharer as well in the glory to be revealed" (5:1), then elders in the congregations have this responsibility and this privilege in double measure, and so too does Peter.[12]

The form of Peter's advice to elders in 5:1–5 recalls the form of the household duty codes in 2:18–25 and 3:1–7, except that here he begins not with those who are subservient

From Present to Future

but with those in positions of leadership and in fact concentrates most of his attention on them. In the Greco-Roman household, Peter was concerned with those who were subordinate and powerless. In the case of slaves and slaveowners he addressed eight verses to slaves and none to their owners. In the case of wives and husbands he addressed six verses to wives and only one to husbands. In the Christian congregation, or "household of God," Peter is more concerned with those in power, for their leadership and example will be a key factor in the congregation's response to the "fiery ordeal" (4:12) and the threat of "your opponent, the devil . . . on the move like a roaring lion" (5:8). He therefore devotes four verses to "elders," just half a verse (5:5a) to "younger ones," and a final half verse (5:5b) to the mutual responsibilities of both groups.

These directives to elders in Asia Minor recall the farewell speech of Paul in the Book of Acts to the elders of Ephesus at the port of Miletus (Acts 20:17–38). Paul had said, "Take heed to yourselves and to all the flock in which the Holy Spirit has made you guardians. Be shepherds to the church of God, which he bought with his own blood" (Acts 20:28). Peter, in the same vein, urges the elders, "Shepherd the flock of God that is in your care" (1 Pet 5:2a), adding that these pastoral duties must be performed "not out of compulsion but willingly before God" (v 2b). The contrast is not between duty and free choice, but between a sense of duty based on one's own ego and a sense of duty based on the will of God. Peter knows that the human ego is by far the more severe taskmaster, and the experience of too many ministers today bears him out. Possibly he speaks out of his own experience. In any event he wants the ministry of elders to be a free and joyful response to the love of God, not a compulsive act of self-gratification. Because money is the commonest measure of self-gratification, he adds that greed cannot and must not be their motivation. They must minister to their people "not greedily but with enthusiasm" (v 2c). Their incentive "before God" must come from within—from their own hearts and wills—not from the anticipation of material rewards.

Most important of all, elders must not "lord it over your respective congregations, but be examples to the flock" (5:3). Peter himself has set the example. He does not lord it over them by "talking down" to them as an apostle—his initial self-identification as "apostle of Jesus Christ" in 1:1 was sufficient to make the point—but as their "fellow elder" (5:1) makes them his peers and colleagues. Their responsibility is to treat the congregations under their care in the same way. Peter also has in mind the model of Christian leadership that Jesus held before his disciples as they approached Jerusalem. Perhaps he is remembering Jesus' words as recorded in Mark: "You know that those considered rulers among the Gentiles lord it over them, and their great ones exercise authority over them. That is not how it is among you: whoever wants to be great among you will be your servant, and whoever wants to be first among you will be the slave of all" (Mark 10:42–44). Peter is not quite so radical in addressing the elders of Asia Minor as Jesus had been with him and the other disciples. He does not tell the elders they have to be "slaves." Yet the principle is the same. If the elders want their people to be "servants" of God and of Jesus Christ (cf. 2:16), they themselves must be "examples" of servant-hood, not of power or self-assertion.

The accent on servanthood guarantees that the principle of mutuality expressed in 1 Pet 4:7–11 is not violated in 5:1–5. As soon as he tells the "younger" (i.e., the members of each congregation) to "defer to the authority of elders," Peter hastens to add, "All of you with each other, then, clothe yourselves with humility, for God 'opposes the arrogant, but gives grace to the humble'" (5:5). Nor has Peter forgotten that the "end of all things is near" (4:7). When he promises

89   From Present to Future

to faithful elders an "unfading crown of glory" at the time the "chief shepherd" appears (v 4), he is not promising them anything different from the hope held out to every genuine believer in Christ. The "crown" has nothing to do with the authority to rule, but is more like a victor's wreath made from an unfading flower known as the "amaranth." It represents "praise, glory, and honor at the time when Jesus Christ is revealed" (1:7) and is simply another expression for the "living hope," or the "indestructible, incorruptible, and unfading inheritance reserved in heaven" for all who love Christ and await his coming. Elders gain their "crown" in the same way as everyone else in the congregation, by doing what they were called to do (cf. 2:21, 3:9).

To "elder" and "younger" alike, Jesus Christ will come as "chief shepherd," for all have shared in the common experience of "going astray like sheep" and all have "turned now to the Shepherd and Guardian of your souls" (2:25). No room is left for the pride of one group over against the other. Only in showing humility toward one another, Peter implies, is it possible to "humble yourselves under the mighty hand of God" (5:6). Without such humility, we would be bowing down to a mere abstraction. God, the God of the future, is most real to us now in the persons of those involved with us in the family of God and engaged with us in the work of ministry: our husbands, our wives, our children and our parents, our "elders" and our "flock."

Whether in the literal household or in the metaphorical "brotherhood" of Christian believers, we find ourselves poised between present and future. We are accountable to the Christ, the "chief shepherd," when he comes, and because we are, we are accountable to each other even now. We draw consolation from "the God of all grace" in the hope that "when it is time he will lift you up" and will "prepare, support, strengthen and establish" us (5:6, 10). In the meantime, Peter's vision is of Christians doing these things for one another in the ministry of elders and in the varied ministries of all who exercise their spiritual gifts "as good managers of God's diversified grace" (4:10). If we are involved individually in a pilgrimage in the footsteps of Jesus Christ to the throne of God, we are corporately the recipients of God's future grace at work even now in the family of God. In one sense we are moving toward the future on the dangerous path of discipleship in a hostile world. In another sense that same future comes to us, for Peter sees its dawning in the shared life and worship and the mutual ministries of Christian households and congregations.

5   THE FUTURE: WHEN FAITH BECOMES SIGHT

The preceding chapter was a long one because present and future are so dynamically intertwined in Peter's thought and language. Throughout most of 1 Peter the future is a "forthcoming" future—to use Bruce Malina's terminology once again—not an "imaginary" future.[1] Either the future grows inevitably out of the present circumstances of Christian discipleship, or else it makes itself evident in advance in the present circumstances of Christian ministry and worship. But what of the "imaginary" future in 1 Peter? In the first place, there is reason to quarrel with the term. Though Peter knows of an ultimate and truly *final* future to the plan of God, he in no way regards it as "imaginary." On the contrary, he seems consciously to curb his imagination so as to speak of the ultimate future only with the greatest caution and restraint.

The revelation

Peter takes deeply to heart a traditional saying of unknown origin: "The eye has not seen, the ear has not heard, nor has it come up in the human heart what God has prepared for those who love him." Paul had quoted this saying in 1 Cor 2:9, adding as his own comment, "But God has revealed it to us by the Spirit" (v 10). To Paul the traditional saying refers to "God's hidden wisdom" (v 7), the mystery of the cross of Christ. Peter, like several other early Christian writers,[2] applies it instead to the unseen and unimagined future in store for believers in Jesus Christ. The decisive "revelation" in 1 Peter is future, not present. The time "when Jesus Christ is revealed" (1 Pet 1:7, 13) or "when his glory is revealed" (4:13, 5:1) is the object of hope, just beyond the horizons of present experience. Even salvation is not yet our full possession but is something "about to be revealed at the last day" (1:5).

All these things, as pointed out in the preceding chapter, belong to the "forthcoming" future. Peter sees intimations of the future "glory" even in the most distressing of present circumstances (4:14). Christians already are following in the footsteps of the unseen Christ to the cross and to heaven (2:21, 3:18). The process of "growing up to salvation" (2:2) is well under way. Yet there is also a measure of reserve about Peter's vision of the future that is not characteristic of most of the "revelatory" or "apocalyptic" literature in Judaism and early Christianity. In certain respects the future remains "imaginary," but because Peter is not so bold as to "imagine" it in all its visible splendor—as John does, for example, in Rev 21–22—he leaves it a mystery. The notion of a future "time when Jesus Christ is *revealed* (1:7, 13) implies that for now he is invisible even to those who believe: "You have never seen him, but you love him. Even now, without seeing, you believe in him" (1:8). He who "appeared in the last of the ages for your sake" (1:20) has disappeared again from human view, having "gone to heaven" and taken his place "at the right hand of God" (3:22). The great future hope in 1 Peter is not so much for a "coming" of the Christ who is distant as for a "revealing" or "unveiling" of the Christ now hidden from our eyes.[3] In that "revealing" will be found the fullness of the "grace" now experienced in bits and pieces (1:13; cf. 4:10) and the full realization of "praise, glory, and honor" for those who had been faithful in moments of trial (1:7; cf. 4:14).

Peter never ventures to explain or describe what this will mean concretely for those who await this "revelation." All that matters is that they will see the Christ whom they now love and worship in faith. The hope of Christians in 1 Peter is not unlike the hope expressed by the author of 1 John: "Beloved, now we are God's children, and what we shall become has not yet been disclosed. We only know that when he appears we shall be like him, because we shall see him as he really is" (1 John 3:2).

The accent on "revelation" is a notable feature of apocalyptic writings. "Apocalypse," in fact, means "revelation." Peter's vision of the future is in some respects reminiscent of contemporary Jewish and Christian apocalypses, and in other respects quite different. In the Jewish apocalypse of *4 Ezra*, dating from a generation or two after 1 Peter, God promises that "the time will come when . . . the city which now is not seen shall appear, and the land which is now hidden shall be disclosed. And everyone who has been delivered from the evils that I have foretold shall see my wonders. For my son the Messiah shall be revealed with those who are with him" (*4 Ezra* 7.28; cf. 12.32; 13.26, 32).[4] According to another passage, "Just as no one can explore or know what is in the depths of the sea, so no one on earth can see my son or those who are with him, except in the time of his day" (*4 Ezra* 13.52). The apocalypse known as *2 Baruch* speaks of a heavenly temple which is not "this building that is in your midst now" but "that which will be revealed, with me, that which was already prepared from the moment I decided to create Paradise" (*2 Bar* 4.2–3). It also promises faithful Jews that they will "see that world which is now invisible to them, and they will see a time which is now hidden to them" (51.8). When God establishes an eternal kingdom in this new world, "then joy will be revealed and rest will appear" (73.1).

1 Peter shares with these apocalyptic writings an interest in that which is "revealed" at the last day, but differs from them in two ways. First, the apocalyptic visions contemplate the revealing not just of a person—the Messiah, or deliverer of the people of God—but a whole mythology: a "city," a "land," a "temple," indeed a new "world." In 1 Peter it is Jesus Christ and him alone who is revealed. Peter leaves the rest to the imaginations of his readers. Second, in apocalyptic literature, whether Jewish or Christian, the "revelation" is not only future but present as well. The very genre of the work is based on the assumption that the prophet or seer who is writing has already been granted a supernatural glimpse of the wonderful things to come. Indeed, the author of *2 Baruch* addresses God as "the one who reveals to those who fear that which is prepared for them so that you may comfort them. You show your mighty works to those who do not know. You pull down the enclosure for those who have no experience and enlighten the darkness, and reveal the secrets to those who are spotless, to those who subjected themselves to you and your Law in faith" (*2 Bar* 54.4–5).

In 1 Peter, by contrast, Jesus Christ and he alone is "revealed." At most, Peter can speak of "glory" or "salvation" or "joy" being revealed along with Christ, but there is no city, no temple, no visions of a land or a new world. Peter, moreover, does not take on himself the role of a prophet or seer who is privileged to see the "revelation" in advance.[5] If he is indeed Peter, he has seen the earthly Jesus, but, in regard to Jesus as he will be "revealed" at the last day, Peter has no edge on his readers. What he says to them he could just as easily have said to himself: "You have never seen him, but you love him. Even now, without seeing, you believe in him, [and] you will rejoice" (1:8). The "revelation" hidden from the eyes of prophets and angels (vv 10-12) is hidden from Peter's eyes as well. 1 Peter contains apocalyptic themes in that it looks to the revealing of Jesus Christ as the solution to the aggravations and tensions facing Christians in the Roman Empire. Yet it is not an "apocalypse" or an essentially "apocalyptic" work. The "apocalypse," or "revealing" of Jesus Christ," is not something that happens now in the visions of a prophet, as in the Book of Revelation (1:1), or in the calling of a missionary, as it was for Paul (Gal 1:2). It is rather the object of hope, not for a gifted few, but for all who love Jesus. This author has seen no visions. He walks by faith and not by sight, and urges his readers to do the same.

Inexpressible joy

"Salvation" and "glory" at the last day then are objective realities in 1 Peter. They are words to describe what God will finally do for his people. The "praise, glory, and honor" of 1 Pet 1:7 simply expands on the single word "glory" to summarize the vindication for which suffering believers patiently wait. But "joy" or "delight" is something different. It is a *subjective* reality. "Joy" is not what God does for us, but rather what we feel or experience as a result of what he has done for us. This too belongs to Peter's "imaginary" or "final" future.

The note of joy is almost as conspicuous in 1 Peter as in Paul's letter to the Philippians.[6] The words of the King James Version echo in the old gospel hymn:

> I have found the joy no tongue can tell
> How its waves of glory roll!
> It is like a great o'erflowing well,
> Springing up within my soul.
>
> It is joy unspeakable and full of glory,
> Full of glory, full of glory;

The Future: When Faith Becomes Sight

It is joy unspeakable and full of glory,
Oh, the half has never yet been told.[7]

In the hymn, and in the King James Version, "joy unspeakable and full of glory" is the believer's present possession. In 1 Peter itself, however, the accent is on future, not present, joy. Having mentioned "a salvation about to be revealed at the last day" (1:5), Peter adds, "Then you [will] rejoice" (1:6) and concludes that "you [will] rejoice with inexpressible and glorious delight when you each receive the outcome of your faith, your final salvation" (1:8b-9).[8] The present is a time of suffering affliction, at least "for a little" (1:6, 5:10), and a time for "faith" in the sense of patient endurance (1:6-7).

Although the message of 1 Peter has frequently been characterized as a message of "joy in suffering," Peter is enough of a realist to know that in the human situation suffering *in itself* is not a cause for joy. He is no masochist. The most he will say about present joy is, "to the extent that you share in the sufferings of Christ, be glad, so that when his glory is revealed you may rejoice all the more" (4:13). Christians can "be glad" not because they are suffering but because they know that when they suffer they are following in the footsteps of Jesus Christ. The only suffering that can be a cause for gladness is suffering "unjustly," or "for doing good," because these were the circumstances of Jesus' suffering. And even this "gladness" is not the "inexpressible joy" of the last day. Peter has two words for joy: one (Greek, *chairein*) for the gladness or consolation of sharing the lot of Jesus Christ and the other (Greek, *agalliasthai*) for the unspeakable delight or jubilation of seeing Jesus face to face at his "revelation." Joy in its most profound sense in 1 Peter is a mystery for it belongs to that "imaginary" (yet unimagined) future still hidden from human view. Joy is by far the most fascinating aspect of that future, and Peter speaks of it only with hesitation and wonder.

Some of our finest Christian writers have caught the note of mysterious joy in the Christian message, whether from 1 Peter or the New Testament generally or their own experience. C. S. Lewis speaks of "approaching the source from which those arrows of Joy had been shot at me ever since childhood."[9] Flannery O'Connor, suffering from the lupus that was to take her life, wrote in 1956 to a friend, "Picture me with my ground teeth stalking joy—fully armed too as it's a highly dangerous quest. The other day I ran up on a wonderful quotation: 'The dragon is at the side of the road watching those who pass. Take care lest he devour you! You are going to the Father of souls, but it is necessary to pass by the dragon.' That is Cyril of Jerusalem instructing catechumens."[10] She captured the spirit not only of Cyril, but of Peter as well.

Even more eloquently, Gilbert K. Chesterton concluded *Orthodoxy*, his great work of Christian apologetics, with this paragraph:

> Joy, which was the small publicity of the pagan, is the gigantic secret of the Christian. And as I close this chaotic volume I open again the strange, small book from which all Christianity came; and I am again haunted by a kind of confirmation. The tremendous figure which fills the Gospels towers in this respect, as in every other, above all the thinkers who ever thought themselves tall. His pathos was natural, almost casual. The Stoics, ancient and modern, were proud of concealing their tears. He never concealed His tears; He showed them plainly on his open face at any daily sight, such as the far sight of His native city. Yet He concealed something. Solemn supermen and imperial diplomatists are proud of restraining their anger. He never restrained His anger. He flung furniture down the front steps of the Temple, and asked

men how they expected to escape the damnation of Hell. Yet He restrained something. I say it with reverence; there was in that shattering personality a thread that must be called shyness. There was something that He hid from all men when he went up a mountain to pray. There was something that He covered up constantly by abrupt silence or impetuous isolation. There was some one thing that was too great for God to show us when He walked upon our earth; and I have sometimes fancied that it was His mirth."[11]

The intriguing suggestion that the "Messianic secret" in the ministry of Jesus was joy is a good point at which to take leave of Peter and his remarkable vision of past, present, and future in the plan of God and in the life of the people of God.

6 CONCLUSION: THE MESSAGE OF
1 PETER TODAY

What remains is the more formidable task of assessing the testimony of 1 Peter to the Christian "brotherhood throughout the world" (5:9) now, nineteen centuries after it was written. This is a task that individual readers and Christian communities must decide for themselves. A commentator can try to describe or recapture what an ancient writer has done. If the writing is Holy Scripture, as 1 Peter is, the commentator may want to bear his own testimony as to what its implications are for the very different world in which we live. The commentator deserves a hearing because he has "paid his dues" by virtue of a long and careful involvement with the text. But in the end, it is not the commentator (scholarly or otherwise) who decides what 1 Peter has to say to us today. It is the people of God who must decide, people who are presumably not so different from the first-century slaves, wives, and husbands of Asia Minor to whom the letter was first written.

The expression "priesthood of all believers" has undergone some significant changes since 1 Peter was written. Luther and the Protestant Reformation adapted this term from the language of 1 Pet 2:5, 9, applying it to the right of every Christian to interpret Scripture in the light of individual conscience and the leading of the Holy Spirit. Peter would not have been sympathetic to the individualizing of his imagery of priesthood, but he would have appreciated the notion that the task of interpreting the will of God and the word of God rests with the people of God, not with a hierarchy of either bishops or highly trained scholars.

This is all the more true of a document like 1 Peter itself, in which so much of the content has to do with the people of God, their identity, and their responsibilities to God, each other, and the world. For Christians to interpret 1 Peter for today is to engage in self-definition. It is not simply to ask, "What does this old book mean?" It is to ask the far more immediate and urgent questions, "Who are we? Where did we come from? What is our calling in this world? What is our role in American life? Where are we going?" All that I offer here are one man's reflections on these universal questions. They are the product of my exegetical study of the text, but inevitably the product as well of my own experience and religious convictions. It could hardly be otherwise.

If 1 Peter is "Protestant" in initiating its own distinctive version of the "priesthood of all believers," it is "Catholic" in the sense that it is one of the earliest of Christian encyclical letters (i.e., a circular letter to a large segment of the church). Only Acts 15:23–29 and the letter of James can claim even the possibility of being older. Moreover, it is the first encyclical from the Roman church and is attributed to the man regarded in Roman Catholic tradition as the first bishop of Rome. It stands as evidence that Peter was indeed in Rome in the first century and played a significant role in the life of that church. Yet its perspective on the institutionalization of religion is more "anabaptist" than Catholic—or Protestant, for that matter. Despite the "respect" or "honor" urged toward the state in 1 Peter, this letter is resistant to any formal establishment of religion. "Respect" is due the emperor as a human being and a human magistrate, but "reverent fear" is for God alone (2:17), the God of Israel and the Father of Jesus Christ.

It is likely that this reserve about institutions would have been maintained even in a Christian empire. The kind of civic religion that identifies or mixes the values of, say, American culture with Christian faith or with the teaching of Jesus Christ finds little support in this letter. For example, the efforts of Billy Graham and the Nixon administration on July 4, 1970, to adapt Peter's "honor the emperor" into "honor America" or "honor the nation" may have been good for American patriotism in a troubled time, but were hardly true to the intentions of 1 Peter itself. It is one thing to urge "respect for the emperor" in a general sense, but it would have been quite another for Peter to initiate an "Honor the Empire" festival or even to sanction participation in such a festival proclaimed by the imperial authorities in Rome or Asia Minor. Such "honor" would have been far too religious, too close to "reverent fear" for this author, and it is doubtful that he would have viewed things any differently in twentieth-century America.

In this sense, 1 Peter is an "anabaptist" work. The "church" (if Peter were to use that word) is a believers' church in that its membership is made up not of people born into a particular religious tradition, but of people "born anew" who have "purified their souls" by faith in God through Jesus Christ (1:21, 22). Because of their conversion experience, they have no vested interest in Roman society or its institutions. This remains true even though Peter urges respect for that society and those institutions. He insists that Christians are not, and must not be, out to destroy the Roman Empire or the Roman household. It is not their role to subvert either the practice of slavery or the traditional husband-wife relationship in the household. They are not to be "busybodies"

Conclusion: The Message of 1 Peter Today

(4:15) spying out other people's behavior or legislating other people's morality. Their role is to respect their fellow citizens in the framework of existing institutions and live in such a way that their fellow citizens might in turn respect them and be drawn to their new faith. There are no formulas for social reform in 1 Peter, only the hope of life and salvation "at the time when Jesus Christ is revealed." For a Social Gospel, one must look to the Old Testament and to other parts of the New.

It would be easy to conclude from all this that 1 Peter is both otherworldly and highly individualistic. When read in this way it calls those who want to be "saved" or "born again" into a life of private piety and individual witness. It is indeed tempting to view 1 Peter as an otherworldly statement of Christian faith, centering on the redeemed individual, the rejection of life in the world, and an individualistic hope of heaven. Such an outlook is summed up in the words of the old gospel song (cited from memory):

This world is not my home, I'm just a-passing through;
My treasures are laid up somewhere beyond the blue;
The angels beckon me from heaven's open door,
And I can't feel at home in this world anymore.

It is not hard to think of passages in 1 Peter on which such lyrics might have been based (e.g., 1:1, 3-4, 17-19; 2:11), and yet the individualistic and otherworldly perspective of the old song must be recognized as far from Peter's intention.

The difference lies in the fact that Christians, despite having no vested interest in the social or political order in Rome or in America, are themselves a social order in 1 Peter, a "people," and not merely an assortment of "saved" individuals. Peter views them as "a chosen race, the King's priesthood, a holy nation, a people destined for vindication" (2:9). He establishes their identity on the basis of ancient Jewish stories and the ancient Jewish Scriptures. They are "honorary Jews," a new Israel, yet somehow without displacing the old. Like the Jews in the Roman Empire (and in many other cultures) they are "aliens and strangers" (2:11), "a chosen people living as strangers in the diaspora" (1:1). Their place—our place—in human society according to Peter is not unlike that described by an anonymous Christian writer a century later:

> For the distinction between Christians and other people is neither in land nor language nor customs. For they do not dwell in cities in some place of their own, nor do they use any strange variety of dialect, nor practice any extraordinary kind of life. . . . Yet while living in Greek and barbarian cities, according as each obtained his lot, and following the local customs, both in clothing and food and in the rest of life, they show forth the wonderful character of their own citizenship. They dwell in their own fatherlands, but as sojourners in them. They share all things as citizens, and suffer all things as strangers. Every foreign country is their fatherland, and every fatherland is a foreign country. . . . They pass their time on the earth, but they have their citizenship in heaven. They obey the appointed laws, and they surpass the laws in their own lives. They love everyone and are persecuted by everyone. They are unknown and they are condemned. They are put to death and they gain life. . . . To put it shortly, what the soul is in the body, the Christians are in the world. The soul is spread through all the members of the body, and Christians throughout the cities of the world. The soul dwells in the body, but is not of the body, and Christians dwell in the world, but are not of the world.[12]

This ancient quotation is far truer to the vision of 1 Peter than the lyrics of "This World Is Not My Home."

The familiar rendering of 1 Pet 2:9 in the King James Version, "a peculiar people," though inaccurate in its own time and even more misleading today, still captures something of the strangeness with which the world perceives Christians when they live as God called them to live. It is akin to the strangeness and suspicion with which many societies have viewed the Jews. Peter's appreciation of the basic "Jewishness" even of Gentile Christian communities in his world holds out the possibility of the building of new bridges between Jew and Christian even today.

Beyond this, the people of God in 1 Peter are also a pilgrim people following in the footsteps of Jesus Christ. Here again 1 Peter stands in—or rather *behind*—the anabaptist tradition. More than any other New Testament writer, Peter combines the emphasis of Paul and the Gospel of John on *believing* in Jesus Christ with that of Jesus himself (as presented in the Synoptic Gospels) on *following* him as disciples in the way of the cross. He achieves in this respect a balance found nowhere else in the New Testament. It is possible to imagine 1 Peter as a letter that Paul might have written if he had paid more explicit attention to the teaching of Jesus, or a letter that Mark, Matthew, or Luke might have written if they had adopted the letter form. Where 1 Peter goes beyond the gospels is in showing that the pilgrimage of discipleship, like the pilgrimage of Jesus, leads past the cross to the resurrection, and finally to the presence of the God of Israel. It is like the journey to the heavenly Jerusalem in the letter to the Hebrews (e.g., Heb 12:22–24; 13:14), except that Peter has little interest in the splendor and trappings of a heavenly city or temple. What matters is that it is a pilgrimage toward the experience of seeing Jesus face to face and, therefore, a pilgrimage toward joy.

NOTES

Chapter 2   The Past: Claiming a Heritage

1. Joseph Campbell, *The Power of Myth* (New York: Doubleday, 1988), 15.

2. C. S. Lewis, *Miracles* (New York: Macmillan, 1948), 161, n. 1.

3. For a literary development of this theme, read the short story, "The River," by Flannery O'Connor, in *A Good Man Is Hard to Find* (New York: Harcourt Brace, 1955).

4. G. Vermes, *The Dead Sea Scrolls in English* (Harmondsworth, England: Penguin, 1962), 239.

Chapter 3   The Present: Living in a Hostile Society

1. See the second-century *Martyrdom of Polycarp*, especially chs 13–17.

2. Amos Niven Wilder, "To Pulpit and Tribune," in *Grace Confounding* (Philadephia: Fortress, 1972), 46.

3. See, e.g., 2 Macc 7:34–36: "But you, unholy wretch, you most defiled of all men, do not be elated in vain and puffed up by uncertain hopes, when you raise your hand against the children of heaven. You have not yet escaped the judgment of the almighty, all-seeing God. For our brothers after enduring a brief suffering

have drunk of ever-flowing life under God's covenant; but you, by the judgment of God, will receive just punishment for your arrogance." See also 2 Macc 7:17, 19, 31; 4 Macc 9:5, 10:11.

Chapter 4   From Present to Future

1. Bruce J. Malina, "Christ and Time: Swiss or Mediterranean?" *Catholic Biblical Quarterly* 51.1 (1989): 1–31.

2. See ibid., 10–17.

3. Ibid., 5–6.

4. Gerard Manley Hopkins, "God's Grandeur," in *A Little Treasury of Modern Poetry* (New York: Scribner's, 1946), 45.

5. The word commonly translated "prison" (Greek, *phylakē*) is different from the words used in 2 Pet 2:4; Jude 6; and the Enoch literature for the imprisoned "angels who sinned" before the flood, and the same as that used in Rev 18:2, where Babylon is said to be a "haunt" or "refuge" for "every unclean spirit" as well for "every unclean and hateful bird."

6. Cf. the "three unclean spirits, like frogs," provoking the "kings of the whole world" to assemble for battle at Armageddon, according to Rev 16:13–14.

7. *Treatise on the Resurrection*, 45.25–28, attributed to Valentinus or one of his disciples in the second century (B. Layton, *The Gnostic Treatise on Resurrection from Nag Hammadi* [Missoula, MT: Scholars Press, 1979], 17).

8. From the poem, "God's Grandeur," cited above in note 4.

9. Flannery O'Connor, *The Habit of Being* (New York: Farrar/ Straus/Giroux, 1979), 367.

10. Clement of Alexandria, *Stromateis*, or "Miscellanies," bk 3, ch 10, in *Alexandrian Christianity*, ed. J. E. L. Oulton and H. Chadwick (Philadelphia: Westminster Press, n.d.), 71.

11. Cited from Augustine in *Patrologia Latina*, 35.2025, by Paul Hinnebusch, *Friendship in the Lord* (Notre Dame, IN: Ave Maria Press, 1974), 116–17.

12. "Witness" here does not mean "eyewitness" of the actual sufferings of Jesus. Peter was in any case *not* an eyewitness of Jesus' crucifixion according to the gospels, but like the other disciples deserted Jesus at the time of his arrest (cf. Mark 14:50). "Witness"

refers rather to *anyone* who bears testimony to the gospel of salvation through Jesus' death.

Chapter 5   The Future: When Faith Becomes Sight

1. Bruce J. Malina, "Christ and Time: Swiss or Mediterranean?" *Catholic Biblical Quarterly* 51.1 (1989): 10–17.

2. Notice, e.g., the echoes of this saying in *1 Clem.* 34.8; *2 Clem.* 11.7; and *Mart Pol.* 2.3.

3. Cf. John 16:16, "A little while, and you will see me no more; and again a little while, and you will see me."

4. These quotations from Jewish apocalyptic writings are taken from J. H. Charlesworth, ed., *The Old Testament Pseudepigrapha*, vol. 1 (Garden City, NY: Doubleday, 1983).

5. Even if he had been a prophet, he would not have had this privilege. In his view, the only thing "revealed" to the ancient prophets was actually a nonrevelation: i.e., that the messages they brought were "not for their own benefit but for yours" (1:12).

6. See G. F. Hawthorne, "The Note of Joy," in *Philippians*, Word Biblical Themes (Waco, TX: Word, 1987), 107–10.

7. *Inspiring Hymns* (Grand Rapids: Singspiration, 1951).

8. William Tyndale straddled the fence in his 1534 edition of the New Testament (reprinted by Cambridge University Press in 1939) by making the rejoicing future in 1:6 ("in the which tyme ye shall reioyce") but present in 1:8 ("ye beleue, and reioyce with ioye vnspeakable and glorious").

9. C. S. Lewis, *Surprised by Joy: The Shape of My Early Life* (New York: Harcourt, Brace & World, 1955), 230.

10. Flannery O'Connor, *Collected Works* (New York: Library of America, 1988), 979.

11. G. K. Chesterton, *Orthodoxy* (New York: John Lane, 1931), 298–99.

Chapter 6   Conclusion: The Message of 1 Peter Today

1. *Epistle to Diognetus* 5.1–2, 4–5, 9–12; 6.1–3.

INDEX OF SCRIPTURES

Index

INDEX OF SCRIPTURES